ARISTOTLE'S
ART OF POETRY

ARISTOTLE'S
ART OF POETRY

A GREEK VIEW OF
POETRY AND DRAMA

WITH AN INTRODUCTION AND EXPLANATIONS

BY

W. HAMILTON FYFE

PRINCIPAL AND VICE-CHANCELLOR,
UNIVERSITY OF ABERDEEN

OXFORD
AT THE CLARENDON PRESS

Oxford University Press, Ely House, London W.1

GLASGOW NEW YORK TORONTO MELBOURNE WELLINGTON
CAPE TOWN SALISBURY IBADAN NAIROBI LUSAKA ADDIS ABABA
BOMBAY CALCUTTA MADRAS KARACHI LAHORE DACCA
KUALA LUMPUR HONG KONG

FIRST EDITION 1940
REPRINTED 1948, 1952, 1957, 1961, 1963, 1966

PRINTED IN GREAT BRITAIN

TABLE OF CONTENTS

NOTE

THE translation here used is that of Ingram
Bywater, which the editor, a Satyr to his
Hyperion, has ventured to alter slightly in a
few places.

INTRODUCTION

THE *Poetics* of Aristotle has a long and famous life, which began about 330 B.C. In later Greek and in Latin literature, although there are traces of its influence, we do not hear much of it. In the Middle Ages it was known and amply misunderstood by Syrian and Arabic scholars. Its modern life begins in Italy at the end of the fifteenth century. Since then it has been translated and edited and annotated in every century and in many languages, attaining at times the authority of a holy writ, the doctrines of which were received with more reverence than understanding. It is still alive, because it is a study of a great art by a peculiarly acute, learned, and methodical critic. It is the first work of literary criticism and it is written by the world's first scientist.

Aristotle was born in 384 B.C. at Stagira (Stavros) in Chalcidice at the north end of the Aegean Sea and about forty miles east of Salonika. His father was court physician to King Amyntas of Macedon, a fact to which Aristotle owed his association with Alexander the Great and his habit of viewing all subjects from the angle of biology. Indeed he had medical traditions through his mother also; dissection was in his blood. At the age of seventeen he began what we should call his University education and studied for twenty years at Plato's 'Academy'. Then after five years of travel and teaching among the Aegean islands and in Asia Minor he was chosen by King Philip of Macedon as tutor to his son, Alexander, aged thirteen. He held this post for seven years,

during which he doubtless developed the encyclo-
paedic scope of his interest and a method of exposition
both lucid and didactic. Alexander had as his tutor
the most learned of then living men, perhaps the most
learned of all men. How much he profited is doubtful. It may have been Aristotle's influence that
turned a semi-barbarian into something like a Greek.
Alexander promoted an edition of the Iliad and was
accompanied on his campaigns by Greek historians
and scholars, and his policy of colonization spread
Greek culture widely in the Near East, with the
result that Alexandria became the intellectual centre
of the world. But his taste seems to have been
rather for romantic legend than for systematic
scholarship. In the science of his strategy perhaps
he owed a debt to his tutor. If so, we may note a
parallel in many centuries. It is for purposes of war-
fare that princes have usually encouraged science;
democracies in this respect are no less princely.

In 335 B.C. Aristotle returned to Athens and
opened the Lyceum, rather as a supplement than as a
rival to the Academy. It was what we should call
a Research Institute, a centre of co-operative study,
where facts and theories were collected and a learned
library assembled. Cloisters were a feature of the
Lyceum building, and Aristotle's school thus got the
name of 'peripatetic' from the Greek word for 'walk-
ing about'. The Emperor Justinian suppressed the
Lyceum 860 years later—an age not yet attained by
any university in Europe.

Ten years later the Athenians, fearful of the power
of Macedon, but emboldened after Alexander's death
to consider means of self-defence, started a spy-hunt.

Aristotle, as Alexander's former tutor, was inevitably suspect. Threatened, it is said, with prosecution for impiety, and fearing the fate of Socrates, he withdrew to Chalcis in Euboea, 'lest Athens should twice sin against philosophy'; and there he died in his sixty-third year, little suspecting, we may suppose, that twenty-one centuries later people with no knowledge of Greek might still be interested in his views on poetry and drama.

The opening words of the work known as Aristotle's *Metaphysics*[1] are 'All men by nature desire to know'. Certainly Aristotle with his colleagues and pupils at the Lyceum lived up to this optimistic view. They took the whole world of knowledge for their field, and Aristotle wrote on Philosophy (metaphysical and moral), Logic, Religion, Oratory, Poetry and Drama, Political Science, History, Zoology, Botany, and Meteorology. His books were of two kinds. What he called his 'exoteric' writings were intended for the educated general public. Many of these were in the form of dialogues and were evidently written with some charm of style, since Cicero praises 'the golden stream of Aristotle's eloquence'. These 'popular' works Aristotle published in his lifetime, but they are all, except in fragments, lost. What we possess are 'esoteric' works, which were probably not published until the first century B.C.[2]   These were

[1] Aristotle's treatise on philosophy was called 'meta ta physica', because in his collected works it came 'after the physics', i.e. after his treatise on natural science. Hence our word 'metaphysics'.

[2] The delay is mysterious. Aristotle apparently left his manuscripts together with the library of the Lyceum to his successor, Theophrastus, and there is a story that more than two centuries later they were discovered in the cellar of a house belonging to the descendants of the friend to whom Theophrastus in turn had bequeathed them.

lectures or lecture-notes or records of discussion, all reverently preserved at the Lyceum. They are not intended for general reading and have therefore little merit of literary form. Their style is plain, practical, compact. He says what he has to say with typical Greek simplicity, and admirably avoids the sesquipedalian verbiage which enshrouds a good deal of later philosophy and criticism. But while his writing is simple, it is often difficult to understand, because Aristotle was a systematic thinker, and since his pupils were assumed to be familiar not only with his terminology and modes of thought, but also with his system as a whole, his lectures on one subject often contain allusions to statements, theories, and conclusions given in other lectures on what seems to us a totally different subject. Thus some of his remarks on poetry are only intelligible to those who have read his lectures on political science and on philosophy. That is why Aristotle's books are proverbially difficult, and need at least some of the explication which commentators have so abundantly supplied. Lecturers' notes are never good reading, and some of the notes included in Aristotle's 'works' may even be those still more tangled puzzles, the notes taken down by a pupil. It is rumoured that the discovery of such a book of notes, left behind by an undergraduate in the lecture-room, caused Dean Inge to relinquish in horror his professorial chair at Cambridge. So we must not blame Aristotle, if we sometimes find his note-books difficult. No one can study any part of his work without feeling in touch with a man of simple, logical intelligence, who knows what he wants to say and, although the notes of his lectures may be cramped and allusive, is well able to express his meaning with lucid force.

The 'desire to know' certainly came to Aristotle by nature and was developed by persistent practice. And in this practice, however widely the subjects of his study differed, his method was the same. To know meant to ask 'What is this? Why is it what it is? And how does it differ from what it isn't?' 'This' might be a fish, or a poem, a part of the human body, a political constitution or a piece of conduct. It was all the same to Aristotle. He wanted to know what this thing really in itself *is*, and what are the relations between it and other things of the same class or kind. So, whatever the thing might be, he proceeded to study it in detail, and tried to analyse it into its component parts. In doing this he distinguished its matter, its form, the power or agent that made it what it is, and its end or purpose, asking (1) What is this made of? (2) Why has it this shape and structure? (3) How did it 'get that way'? (4) And what is it for? We may note in passing that the answer to (4) supplies the clue to (2)—as we say in our woollier language 'the adaptation of the organism is determined by its function'.

The search for an answer to the second question opened his eyes to the process which we know as evolution. Things grow—flowers, fishes, tragic poetry, and city-states. They develop until they reach maturity, realize to the full their inherent capacity and become themselves. This is the method of study with which we are most familiar in the science of biology, and it may seem odd to find it applied to the criticism of poetry and drama and the study of political constitutions. But it is a sound method, which keeps the feet of the inquirer on firm ground.

Moreover, in studying all these widely different objects, he used what we call the method of Induction. He first collected all the available data—and when we consider that he had no instruments for precise observation of natural objects and no systematic historical records, it is amazing how many facts in all these different fields of study he discovered and established. Having assembled the facts, he then proceeded to form a theory, so as to group and explain them under one general idea. Thus before forming his political theories, he collected all the known facts about forms of government; and before tackling in the *Poetics* the theory of poetry and drama, he compiled a list of the plays produced at Athens with the titles of the plays and the names of the author, producer and actors, and the winners of prizes.

In all his study his aim seems to have been largely practical. In Athenian society, with its lack of mechanical devices, there was little opportunity for applying scientific knowledge to practical use. But even in his study of natural science it is clear that he considers accurate knowledge an aid to right living. He did not, like Socrates, identify virtue and knowledge, but while believing that the highest state of human perfection is the contemplation of eternal truth, he admits that the man who knows most is likely to live best. In the fields of moral philosophy and political science his practical aim is clear, and it is even clearer in his treatment of oratory and of poetry. Both his *Rhetoric* and his *Poetics* are practical courses of instruction.

In the *Rhetoric* his object is to formulate the rules for constructing a good speech—a matter of capital importance to every one who took even a small share in the political and social life of Athens. 'What is the object of a speech, the end aimed at?' The answer is 'to persuade an audience'. 'How is that end in fact achieved?' 'By virtue of the style, the argument, the arrangement.' And this leads on to a theory of 'oratorical proof'—how to prove your point in a speech or at any rate appear to prove it—a theory under which the observed facts could be grouped and explained.

The aim of the *Poetics* is equally practical. It is a text-book of instruction. Aristotle tells his class what to seek and what to avoid in the construction of poetic dramas; what is the effect at which such dramas aim; how the achievement of that aim determines the form of the drama; by what means that aim is achieved and by what defects a dramatist may fail to achieve it; what are the charges which critics bring against poets and how such charges may be countered.

The *Poetics* has a further practical aim, an aim which an Athenian would regard as more important than any critical theory of literature. It has a moral aim. Greek writers view all aspects of life and nature under moral concepts. They are predominantly concerned with possible effects on human conduct. Aristotle is therefore anxious to show that the effect of tragedy upon the spectators is something that is good for them, and in proving this he was faced—like those who proclaim that 'Guinness is good for you'—with the contrary opinion of the puritans. Plato, his former master—poet, philosopher, and puritan—distrusted the poet's power to stimulate emotion. We have, he says, a natural desire to weep and wail without restraint. That is a desire which, when real calamity overtakes us, we rightly try to keep in check. Yet by tragic poetry that desire is fed to satiety. 'Poetry waters what we ought to wither'—as if emotion were a weed which could be resolutely kept underground.

Aristotle knew better than that. He was an accurate observer and must have noticed the usual result of sitting on a safety-valve. He knows that emotion must have an outlet, and assigns to dramatic poetry the moral function of providing such an outlet safely, conveniently, and at regular intervals. If people try to bottle up their feelings, the accumulated surplus may explode in violent and irrational conduct. It is the object of tragedy to produce pleasure. (That had never before been explicitly admitted and has since been often forgotten.) But pleasure itself, as Aristotle tells us in his lectures on moral philosophy, is neither good nor bad. It is merely the natural accompaniment of unhindered activity and, according as the activity is good or bad, so is the pleasure which accompanies it. The peculiar pleasure which it is the aim of tragedy to produce is the accompaniment of a good activity, an activity which provides for our emotions 'a good relief'; it releases the surplus which might otherwise dangerously accumulate. As Byron says in one of his letters, using, as befits Byron, a metaphor more lofty but less exact than Aristotle's, 'Poetry is the lava of the imagination, whose eruption prevents an earthquake'.

To-day, as in all centuries, the pleasure we derive from the sadness and horror of a tragic play is the pleasure of vicarious experience. It enables us to feel the thrill of violent emotions, such as find no outlet in the humdrum circumstance of daily life, and could not indeed in any circumstance be aroused in us without disaster and distress to ourselves and our neighbours. The indulgence of such feeling is definitely pleasant. Probably that is the reason why we enjoy tragedy. We do not much consider whether it is good for us or not. But there is comfort in Aristotle's assurance that it is. If the cinema could brew as strong a purge, an Aristotle of the twentieth century might share Plato's doubts. Nightly doses must surely have a debilitating effect on the nervous constitution. But Athenians could witness tragedies only at the annual festivals of Dionysus. They took their purge at regular intervals to keep their emotions in good working order.

A Greekless reader of the twentieth century, when offered a translation of Aristotle's *Poetics*, may well ask, 'What is there here of interest to me?' The answer is 'Much, if you are interested in plays and poetry and novels'. It would be absurd to say, as Lessing said, that, as a critic of literature, Aristotle is 'as infallible as the elements of Euclid'. And even Euclid is outmoded now. But we may justifiably echo the saying of Saintsbury, the historian of criticism, that 'it is impossible for anyone who undertakes the office of a critic to omit the study of Aristotle without very great harm'. Even this sounds like an exaggeration. But it is true, because Aristotle with the plain perspicacity of common sense discovers the fundamental principles of dramatic art, which neither critics nor dramatists can neglect without becoming irrelevant and in-effective.

Before tackling the translation which follows, the inter-chapters in italics which provide a summary, and the notes which offer to explain what may seem obscure, the Greekless reader, for whom this edition is intended, may like to consider in advance the chief merits and defects of the *Poetics*.

We have noted already that Aristotle was the first critic of literature to observe the distinction between moral and aesthetic criteria. He is definite in his view that the aim of tragedy is to give pleasure, a peculiar kind of pleasure which accompanies the release of feeling effected by the stage performance of a tragedy. But does his theory fit the facts? What happens to-day on the rare occasions when we see a great tragedy performed? The human interest holds us. We share the feelings of people like Othello or Macbeth or Maurya in Synge's *Riders to the Sea* or Lavinia Mannon in Eugene O'Neill's *Mourning becomes Electra*. These are all people like ourselves, yet somehow, even in the two modern dramas, raised to a higher power. They achieve a slightly more than human dignity. And yet we fully share their feelings and share them the more easily and exactly because the poet has excluded all those circumstances and con-siderations which in real life confuse our feelings and deny us pleasure. The author embodies his emotion in dramatic form and, as we share it, it becomes our own. If the tragedy has its way with us, our secreted emotion—and perhaps also the bodily secretion of tears—is released, and when the storm of excitement subsides, we are left with a sense of pleasurable relief.

We have the same sense of nervous tension resolved
in pleasurable relief when, distressed by trouble, we
sit down to the piano—or perhaps merely turn on the
gramophone or wireless—and submit to the excitement of great music. In the same way a great poem or
a great picture both excites and relieves our emotions.
Athenian tragedy united all these appeals—poetry,
music, pictorial expression; it carried the yet stronger
and more popular appeal of a thrilling story and
provided in the great outdoor theatre of Dionysus
the intensification of mass psychology. It was indeed
a powerful aperient. People who void their hysterics
by reading slipshod accounts of football and racing,
adultery and murder, might better their health by
means of this safer and much more satisfying form
of relief. It is still available; and great works of art
come so seldom within our reach that there is no
danger of incontinent indulgence.

In prescribing for the proper construction of a
tragedy, one point on which throughout the *Poetics*
Aristotle lays most emphasis is likely to offend modern
readers. 'The first essential', he says, 'the life and
soul, so to speak, of Tragedy is the Plot: character
comes second.' To-day our interest centres on character. We seek to discover in the persons of a play their
psychological complexes and our own. We may even
hope for glimpses into the dark region of 'the uncon-
scious'. This insistence on the prime importance of
plot seems to us trivial, unintellectual. It apparently
ranks a competent piece of stage-craft—*East Lynne*
or *Diplomacy* or *Ten Minute Alibi*—beside or indeed
above the tragedies of Aeschylus or Shakespeare.
Most of us would agree with the dramatist Vanbrugh

that 'the chief entertainment as well as the moral lies much more in the Character and the Diction than in the Business and the Event'. Surely in this matter Aristotle is obsolete! But consider his plain, objective, unemotional common sense, his accurate attention to the known facts, and his firm logic in framing a theory to explain them. The aim of a tragedy is to give the audience a peculiar form of pleasure such as no other art can give, and its success or failure must therefore be judged by reference to that aim. How does the tragedian achieve it? He arouses the emotions of his audience by re-presenting life to them. And this he does by staging a story. In any story there must be people, and they, as human beings, must have moral and intellectual qualities. Each has a character of his own. Therefore the dramatist needs skill in psychology; the character of his persons must react upon the incidents of his story and vice versa. But psychology must be subordinate to his main object, the staging of a story. Character-drawing, music, poetry, scenery, rhetoric, argument—these are fine things in themselves and may become the material of many kinds of art. But what Aristotle has under his microscope is dramatic art; and just as colour is a precious material of plastic art and yet there can be no picture without the form of an outline or design, so too is plot the necessary form of drama. We may say with truth that William James, the psychologist, is a greater artist than Edgar Wallace and provides incomparably better reading. But his books are not novels. Edgar Wallace's 'crook' stories reveal character hardly at all, but they *are* novels or stories, because they have a plot. No plot, no story; and the aim of the tragic artist is to give a peculiar form of pleasure by staging a story. Aristotle's logic is four-square; and his dictum is true to the facts of experience, for, although an audience of intellectuals may derive pleasure from a 'conversational' play that has little or no plot, it is impossible without a close-knit story to produce the true thrill of tragedy and its own peculiar form of emotional release.

Italian critics of the sixteenth century deduced from Aristotle's *Poetics* their famous doctrine of the Three Unities, which demanded from dramatists a crippling ingenuity. By the Unity of Place they meant that there must be in a play no change of scene. Of this Aristotle says nothing: he found no authority for it in the plays he studied. The Unity of Time demands that the period of time imagined to elapse in the play should exactly correspond with the time taken in production. What Aristotle says is that Greek dramatists endeavoured 'to keep as far as possible within a single circuit of the sun or something near that'—a far less rigorous restriction, and moreover not a rule but merely a statement of observed fact.[1] But the Unity of Action he does state as a rule and lays on it the strongest emphasis.

What, he asks, are the qualities of a story that gives us the genuine tragic thrill? Again his answer has the quiet humility of common sense. 'It must have a beginning, a middle, and an end.' This may seem too obvious a dictum, but playwrights and novelists fail and have failed and will fail again for lack of heeding it. And as for length, it must not be so long that the

---

[1] And to the generalization there are exceptions, e.g. Aeschylus' *Eumenides*, Sophocles' *Trachiniae*, and Euripides' *Supplices*.

audience will forget the beginning before they come to the end. Obvious again, yet there are novels and some plays which omit to satisfy the rule; and sermons suffer sometimes from a like defect. One more point he adds: that it must be one story and not several. That looks at first sight equally platitudinous, but it states the principle of organic unity in works of art, and states it, as it were, in words of one syllable beyond all possibility of misconstruction.

Aristotle explains further how to apply this rule of the Unity of Action in the construction of a play. The incidents which are the component parts of the story must be as essential to the whole as are the parts of a living organism, so that no part can be removed or altered without destroying or altering the whole. In a play or story this means that each incident must result either inevitably or at least probably from what has gone before and must—inevitably or at least probably—cause what follows. This causal connexion is essential to the Unity of Action, i.e. to make the story of the play one story and not a mere group of stories. This helps us to understand what Aristotle means when he says that all forms of art are 'modes of imitation'. The artist holds a mirror up to nature. But it is not an ordinary mirror. Neither does it exactly reproduce nor does it distort the objects which confront it; indeed its function is the exact opposite of distortion; it presents a picture in which the confused and therefore unintelligible facts of life are reduced to coherence. It transforms a blur into a picture. And in order to perform this miracle of giving form to chaos, the dramatist's first business is to make his story one coherent whole. He must not cut a slice at

random from real life—not even the most intransigent of 'realists' do that—he must select his
incidents to illustrate his own conception. Ibsen,
speaking of *Ghosts* in one of his letters, says, 'My
object was to make the reader feel that he was
going through a piece of real experience'. It is his
selection and the consequent effect of inevitable
sequence which achieve this.

Experience presents life as an irrational tangle of
incidents. The artist's mirror makes sense of the
tangle and represents life with a pattern distinct in the
threads. What happened to the Joneses in real life
may be material for many stories. A story that 'has
unity' will tell us what must happen or at any rate what
probably would happen, given the character of the
Joneses and the nature of their circumstances. If it
did actually happen, so much the better, for 'what has
happened is obviously possible; otherwise it would not
have happened'. (Had Aristotle a sly sense of humour
or none at all?) It still remains for the dramatist to
show that it could happen and how. His imaginative
'imitation' presents to us not the confused and confusing details but the governing principles of human
life as he descries them; he gives us, in Aristotle's
language, not 'the particular' but 'the universal', and
the pupils who attended Aristotle's lectures on Poetry
would be expected to remember how he had said,
speaking on quite a different subject, that 'the value of
a universal is that it reveals causal connexion'. So we
see that to 'have unity' a story must be 'universal' and
to this end the incidents must be so selected that they
seem to be bound in a strict sequence of cause and
effect. It is selection that gives to art its own reality,

and that is why Aristotle says that poetic drama is something more philosophic or scientific than an accurate calendar of events. It reveals the permanent and universal characteristics of human nature. In short it tells us more about life.

Aristotle's 'doctrine' of the tragic hero[1] is one that puzzles modern readers. He holds that the hero of a truly tragic story must be one who recognizably shares our humanity, yet somehow seems to rise above our level—like the portraits, we might say, of Gainsborough or Reynolds—not a paragon of righteousness, yet a man of justly high repute. And he must fall from prosperity into misfortune not through any vice or villainy such as might morally justify the disaster, but through an error—due no doubt to some intellectual or moral defect—which so far reinforces the malignity of fate that, although he does not deserve his fall, yet his own mistake has fatally caused or helped to cause it. This recipe Aristotle produced according to his habit as a result of inductive research. Having read all the available tragedies, he formed this general conception of the appropriate hero for a tragic story. His conception was inevitably determined by the conditions of theatrical performance at Athens. The Greek actor had to address an audience of many thousands in the open air, wearing, in order to make himself visible and audible, high stilted boots, flowing robes, and a large mask fitted with a megaphone. Realism was impossible; he inevitably looked 'larger than life' and must move and gesticulate with ponderous dignity. Any attempt to bring the persons of the stage to the level of everyday life involved a complete

[1] See Chapter 13, p. 32.

breach with the conventions of the Athenian stage and consequent failure in dramatic effect—just as Shakespeare's effects designed for the 'apron-stage' of the Globe theatre are inevitably modified by modern production on a 'picture-stage'.

But—more perhaps by luck than logic—Aristotle here touches a fundamental truth. The hero of any tragedy—ancient or modern—must be one whom we regard as a fine fellow. He certainly need not be 'of good family' or even 'in high station'—those requirements were peculiar to Greek drama. But he must be 'heroic', as is Macbeth despite his crime; he must be worthy of our interest and regard. Otherwise the play will fail to provide the tragic thrill, as Ibsen's *Rosmersholm* and Galsworthy's *Justice* and Dreiser's *American Tragedy* fail by a small margin, because the hero is in each case rather 'a poor fish'.[1] On the other hand it is obvious that the destruction of a faultless hero, who makes no mistakes, by a force wholly external to himself—Job is a good example—does not stir tragic emotion. There must be something in the hero himself, which obstinately and ironically combines with adverse circumstance, so that at last even his good qualities co-operate with both to fatal issues. As we read or listen to a tragedy, it seems to us equally intolerable and inevitable that such a venial error should start such an avalanche of disaster. It is this which provides the peculiar tragic thrill, and if modern readers feel inclined to question Aristotle's recipe for the provision of this thrill, the defendant can call as witnesses Hamlet and Oedipus, Antigone

[1] Ibsen's *Ghosts* also, powerful and moving though it is, does not give the *peculiar* tragic thrill, because it has no hero at all.

and Lear, Rustum and the Mayor of Casterbridge and Richard Feverel. Against such evidence a prudent judge could only dismiss the case.

Although the hero must fall from happiness to misery, Aristotle does not insist that a tragedy must have an unhappy ending. Indeed he unexpectedly awards the prize to the plot in which at the eleventh hour a fortunate discovery averts the irrevocable act of violence. This shocks many critics; it seems to smack of sentimental weakness. They remember how the German producers of Ibsen's *Doll's House* so persistently altered the ending of the play that the author in self-defence devised for them a happy ending of his own. A similar distaste for unrelieved disaster obliged the Victorian dramatist, Pinero, to alter the ending of *The Profligate*. The distaste for gloomy endings is indeed common and not wholly sentimental. There is a delicious thrill in a reprieve. Most novelists have learned that lesson, perhaps too well. In unskilful hands the happy ending may spoil the true tragic effect. But Aristotle throughout lays insistent emphasis on skill in construction.

There are other outstanding merits in the literary criticism of the *Poetics*, such as the definition of what we call literature in prose or verse, for which Greek has no word; the tracing of poetry to its origin in (1) the natural human instinct to imitate things, which we all observe in monkeys and young children; (2) the natural pleasure of recognizing good mimicry; and (3) the instinct for tune and rhythm as means of expressing and releasing emotion. Other notable features of the *Poetics* are the application of the con-

cept of evolution to the history of drama; and the
subtly simple definition of Fiction as 'the art of telling
lies in the right way'. But even Aristotle was human,
and there are defects in this treatise. What seems to us
one obvious defect is the fact that, as the treatise
stands, it deals rather with Dramatics than Poetics.
Aristotle discusses Epic in comparison with drama
and sums up against it as the less effective art. Lyric
poetry he barely mentions, probably because he regarded it as coming under the category of music, and
music as an art was one of the few things that did not
greatly interest Aristotle. No modern in framing a
theory of poetry would confine his attention to poetic
drama. But tragedy loomed immense in the Greek
literature that Aristotle knew. It included lyric
poetry in its choruses and told the stories of the
Homeric saga more concisely and with more emotional effect than Epic. Aristotle's contemporaries
would certainly have agreed with him that tragedy is
the perfect form of serious poetry, so we should not on
that count pass too severe a sentence of censure.[1]

A more surprising defect is that, although he is the
earliest writer to sketch the historical development of
the drama, he lays no stress on its religious origin. An
advocate might argue that English drama had a
similar origin in church and that an exponent of
Shakespeare may well be aware of the fact yet find no
need to stress it. But here the case is different. The
earliest origins of Greek tragedy are still obscure, but
this is certain, that it was evolved from various forms

[1] The *Poetics*, as we possess it, is incomplete. A second book is known
to have existed, and perhaps another. The discussion of lyric and other
kinds of poetry may be lost.

of religious ritual, such as the mimetic worship of Dionysus, the ritual performed at the graves of Heroes or Demi-gods, the choral hymns to Dionysus, and other forms of choral lyric. Moreover, the 'Spring Dionysia', when tragedies were produced, was a great national and religious festival, and the accepted function of tragedy was to retell the old stories of the Epic saga. And although by Aristotle's time the religious aspect was less obvious and dominant than it was in the days of Aeschylus, Sophocles, and Euripides (the only tragedians whose plays have survived to us), yet tragedy was so much under the influence of its original function that the dramatists still retold the same stories over and over again, seeking at the same time to reinterpret them in the light of a later morality. Occasionally a bold innovator ventured to tap a new vein of fiction by inventing his own plot,[1] but apparently without success. By his favourite process of induction Aristotle assured himself of this important fact, and to explain it we are offered the singularly unconvincing suggestion that these old stories alone fulfil the peculiar requirements of tragedy: no others could be found or invented so well calculated to produce the true tragic effect. One can imagine that a modern dramatist, a conflation, say, of T. S. Eliot and Bernard Shaw, *might* seek to stir emotion by borrowing all his plots from the Old Testament and using them to enforce the morality of the New. But he would find it a grim task, and certainly he would not so limit his choice of material, were he not obliged to do so, as a Greek tragedian was obliged, by the very nature and function and history of his art. Aristotle's

[1] See p. 26, note 2.

theory here remains a puzzle. It is as if a writer on primitive Italian painting, observing that the painters took all their subjects from the Bible, should offer as an explanation that nowhere else could they have found subjects proper for painting. We can only suppose either that the religious function of tragedy was less obvious in the fourth century B.C. than it seems to us, or else that this was another of the very few matters in which Aristotle took no interest.

The weakest feature of the *Poetics* is the treatment of literary style. 'Style', said Cardinal Newman, 'is the shadow of a personality', and Longinus, a later Greek critic (probably of the first century A.D.) hears in the sublime language of great literature 'the true ring of a great soul'. To Aristotle all that would sound sentimental. Just as in considering the subject-matter of tragedy he was not concerned to recognize the dramatists as prophets, whose themes were the major problems of human destiny, and gives no hint that Aeschylus had a sweep and grandeur infinitely greater than his fourth-century successors, so in dealing with style he has no concern with personality or souls. Proceeding, as always, by patient inductive research, he observes that all tragedians in their narrative passages, in dialogue, and in choral lyrics, use what may be called poetic diction. This peculiar phenomenon he proceeds to examine, probing the specimens with conscientious scalpel. The resultant verdict is that tragic poetry, since it is the utterance of beings grander than ourselves, must employ uncommon words such as are not used in ordinary conversation. This serves to heighten the tone. But a style which employed none but unfamiliar words would be an unintelligible jargon. The poet must therefore use a judicious mixture, so that his style may 'be at once clear and not mean'.[1]

This certainly seems to miss the cardinal point that in genuine poetry the diction is not mere 'appliqué'; it is fused with the thought and feeling. It is the poet's inevitable utterance. Whatever words he uses—archaic or obsolete or common—no others would suit his meaning. Wordsworth rightly protested against the stale refinement which had come to be an obstacle to poetic expression, yet even his diction is raised—if only by the use of metre—above the style of ordinary conversation. And in Greek tragedy the 'heightening' of the style by the use of obsolete and unfamiliar diction was part of the religious convention, like the language that is still used in church. Aristotle's explanation is bald and unemotional, it avoids the deeper issues, it may infuriate poets and those to whose emotion poetry makes a powerful appeal, but it is true as far as it goes and as sound as careful observation and analysis can make it.[2] Dr. Johnson said that he who dissects a sunbeam with a prism cannot exhibit the wide effulgence of a summer morn; but scientists employ the prism for other and quite useful purposes.

And here is Aristotle's strength revealed in his weakness. He certainly was not, like Plato, acutely sensitive to the magic and music of words. There are

---

[1] Chapter 22, p. 59.

[2] One might apply the same analysis to the modern mode of music. Musicians, like poets, if they are sensitive to contemporary influence, have something new to say, and since the familiar modes can express only familiar thoughts and feelings, their expression must be 'strange', but not incomprehensible; there must be in their music enough of harmony and melody to appeal to people used to listening to older music.

poems attributed to him and some of them are good. But in criticism his attitude to literature is the cool, objective attitude of the scientist, who while dissecting a frog is rightly blind to its exotic beauty. Of 'inspiration', which for Plato is the essence of poetry, Aristotle never says a word. The soul of poetry and drama lies beyond the reach of his anatomical method, but without any predecessor in the same field he successfully achieved almost all that criticism can achieve on inductive principles by observation, analysis, classification, and generalization. The limited vision of his rather dogmatic common sense—he is the Father of all academic Dons—may seem often inadequate and sometimes irritating, but, as Saintsbury, a professor equally dogmatic and much more sensitive, says in his *History of Criticism*, although in literary criticism we have advanced at some points to farther positions, over most of the ground we are still engaged in consolidating the territory which Aristotle occupied. Any readers who wish to 'check up on' Aristotle's views and to understand them more clearly should take them singly and apply them to examples taken from ancient and modern literature. They would find it a pleasant and profitable recreation.

Those who read this translation with no knowledge of the Greek language and little of Greek literature will want, if their interest is aroused, more information about Greek tragedy and the Greek theatre than it is possible to supply in explanatory notes. A dictionary of Greek mythology, such as is published in the *Everyman* series, will give further explanation of names and stories and allusions. J. T. Sheppard's *Greek*

Tragedy (Cambridge University Press) is a good brief book on the subject. Details of staging, costume, and production can be found in *Stage Antiquities of the Greeks and Romans* by J. T. Allen (Harrap). F. L. Lucas's *Tragedy* (Hogarth Press) and Macneile Dixon's *Tragedy* (E. Arnold) deal admirably with the whole subject.

Those who cannot obtain these or other similar books are sure to get useful advice at the nearest Public Library, and none should fail to borrow thence or to buy for themselves some of the best verse translations of Greek plays, e.g. Gilbert Murray's translations of Euripides, especially *Medea*, *The Trojan Women*, and *The Bacchae*, and his Aeschylus' *Agamemnon* (Allen & Unwin); J. T. Sheppard's *Oedipus Tyrannus* (Cambridge University Press); Miss Melian Stawell's *Iphigeneia in Aulis* (Allen & Unwin). Aristophanes is translated in brilliant 'Gilbertian' verse by B. B. Rogers (G. Bell & Sons).

ARISTOTLE
ON THE ART OF POETRY

1–3. *Aristotle defines Poetry as a kind of 'Imitation'. Perhaps a better translation might be 'expression' or even 'idealization' in the strict meaning of that word. What he means is this. A Poet is a 'maker'. The author of a poem and the author of a scientific treatise both use the same means of expression, i.e. words. But the poem differs from the treatise in that its author 'makes' something. The scientist aims at a purely objective statement of fact. The poet re-presents life as seen through the medium of his own personality. He creates something new. So does the novelist and the dramatist in prose. Aristotle knew nothing of them, but his effort at definition suffers from a difficulty which still troubles us. We have no plain word whereby to distinguish artistic prose, which 'makes' something new, from the objective statement of fact, to which it has less affinity than it has to poetry. But at least we have the term 'literature' which, set in contrast with science, helps us to make that distinction. Greek has no such word, and in the words 'maker' and 'imitator' there lurks a confusing ambiguity. A 'maker' who 'imitates' life in this special sense need not write in verse (e.g. Plato's Dialogues). Nor are all those who write in verse 'imitators' (e.g. Empedocles, who wrote scientific treatises in metre). However, while recognizing that artistic prose writers are in this sense 'poets', Aristotle proceeds to follow common parlance and to use 'poet' for one who 'imitates' in verse.*

Other arts, besides Literature, 'imitate' life, e.g. the arts of painting, of music, of dancing. In these also the

artist re-presents life through the medium of his own personality. We distinguish these 'imitative' arts from each
other by the various means employed. These may be form
and colour or sound or rhythmical posturing or words.
Literature is the art which 'imitates' life in words. Those
who do this are 'poets' whether they write in prose or in
one or many kinds of metre.

To us the word 'imitation' suggests an exact reproduction of visible objects, as in a photograph or in the realistic
scenery with which the modern picture-stage is often cum-
bered. Aristotle's use of the word carries no such suggestion. Realism in that sense was not then born. The
poet reproduces the essentials of life and the emotions
which they have aroused in him. He is no more concerned
with 'photographic' reproduction than is the composer of
a 'pastoral' symphony, who does not try to make a noise
like pigs and cows and chickens but to convey to his hearers
a special atmosphere of feeling, to share with them in the
concert hall the emotions he felt in the country. It is in that
sense that the poet (whether in verse or in prose) communi-
cates his emotion by 'imitating' or recreating life.

A second distinction between various kinds of 'imitation'
turns on the objects represented. They may be idealized or
caricatured or realistically represented. Tragedy idealizes
character, represents its personae as on a higher plane
than that on which our own lives are lived; comedy carica-
tures them.

A third distinction turns on the mode of imitation. Some
poets speak throughout in their own character. Some, like
Homer and Milton, vary the narrative by the introduction
of 'characters' who speak in dialogue. In drama the
'characters' do all the speaking 'as though they were
actually doing the things described'.

1. OUR subject being Poetry, I propose to speak not only of the art in general but also of its species and their respective capacities; of the structure of plot required for a good poem; of the number and nature of the constituent parts of a poem; and likewise of any other matters in the same line of inquiry. Let us follow the natural order and begin with the primary facts.

Epic poetry and Tragedy, as also Comedy, Dithyrambic[1] poetry, and most flute-playing and lyre-playing, are all, viewed as a whole, modes of imitation. But at the same time they differ from one another in three ways, either by a difference of kind in their means, or by differences in the objects, or in the manner of their imitations.

Just as form and colour are used as means by some, who (whether by art or constant practice) imitate and portray many things by their aid, and the voice is used by others; so also in the above-mentioned group of arts, the means with them as a whole are rhythm, language, and harmony—used, however, either singly or in certain combinations. A combination of rhythm and harmony alone is the means in flute-playing and lyre-playing, and any other arts there may be of the same description, e.g. imitative piping.[2] Rhythm alone, without harmony, is the means in the dancer's imitations; for even he, by the rhythms of his attitudes, may represent men's charac-

[1] The dithyramb was originally a hymn to Dionysus probably sung as a solo. By the sixth century it became choral, accompanied by dancing and the flute, and was not necessarily confined to the legends of Dionysus.

[2] Greek music and dancing were more definitely 'imitative' than are the modern arts of music and ballet. Plato calls harp-playing or flute-piping without 'imitative' song or dance mere 'brutish noise'; too vaguely emotional, not sufficiently expressive of character.

ters, as well as what they do and suffer. There is
further an art which imitates by language alone, without harmony, in prose or in verse, and if in verse,
either in some one or in a plurality of metres. This
form of imitation is to this day without a name.[1] We
have no common name for a mime of Sophron or
Xenarchus[2] and a Socratic dialogue; and we should
still be without one even if the imitation in the two
instances were in trimeters or elegiacs or some other
kind of verse—though it is the way with people to
tack on 'poet' to the name of a metre, and talk of
elegiac-poets and epic-poets, thinking that they call
them poets not by reason of the imitative nature of
their work, but indiscriminately by reason of the
metre they write in. Even if a theory of medicine or
physical philosophy be put forth in a metrical form,
it is usual to describe the writer in this way; Homer
and Empedocles,[3] however, have really nothing in
common apart from their metre; so that, if the one is
to be called a poet, the other should be termed a physi-
cist rather than a poet. We should be in the same
position also, if the imitation in these instances were
in all the metres, like the *Centaur* (a rhapsody in a
medley of all metres) of Chaeremon; and Chaeremon

[1] We call it 'literature', for which there is no word in Greek.

[2] The mime was the nearest thing to prose fiction known to the
ancient Greeks. It was something like a *genre* picture, a depiction
—usually humorous—of the scenes and characters of ordinary life.
Sophron's prose mimes are traditionally supposed to have suggested the
dialogue-form to Plato. The XVth Idyll of Theocritus is thought to be
a reproduction in verse of one of Sophron's mimes. He lived in the latter
half of the fifth century. Xenarchus is said to have been his son.

[3] The famous Sicilian philosopher and scientist, born early in the
fifth century, who wrote physical and medical treatises in hexameter
verse.

one has to recognize as a poet.[1] So much, then, as to these arts. There are, lastly, certain other arts, which combine all the means enumerated, rhythm, melody, and verse, e.g. Dithyrambic and Nomic[2] poetry, Tragedy and Comedy; with this difference, however, that the three kinds of means are in some of them all employed together, and in others brought in separately, one after the other. These elements of difference in the above arts I term the means of their imitation.

2. THE objects the imitator represents are actions, with agents who are necessarily either good men or bad—the diversities of human character being nearly always derivative from this primary distinction, since the line between virtue and vice is one dividing the whole of mankind. It follows, therefore, that the agents represented must be either above our own level of goodness, or beneath it, or just such as we are; in the same way as, with the painters, the personages of Polygnotus are better than we are, those of Pauson worse, and those of Dionysius just like ourselves.[3] It is clear that each of the above-mentioned arts will admit of these differences, and that it will become a separate art by representing objects with this point of difference. Even in dancing, flute-playing, and lyre-playing such diversities are possible; and they are also possible in the nameless art that uses language, prose

---

[1] But one cannot in his case 'tack on "poet" to the name of a metre', because he wrote in many. Chaeremon wrote tragedies as well as rhapsodies, i.e. epics. Apparently no one followed his lead in writing epic poetry in a 'medley of metres'.

[2] The nome was a hymn sung in solo to the accompaniment of a lyre.

[3] As modern parallels we might take (1) Gainsborough (2) Hogarth, and (3) any portrait painter who makes what are called 'good likenesses'.

or verse without harmony, as its means; Homer's personages, for instance, are better than we are; Cleophon's are on our own level; and those of Hegemon of Thasos, the first writer of parodies, and Nicochares, the author of the *Deiliad*, are beneath it.[1] The same is true of the Dithyramb and the Nome[2]: the personages may be presented in them with the difference exemplified in the . . . of . . . and Argas, and in the Cyclopses of Timotheus and Philoxenus.[3] This difference it is that distinguishes Tragedy and Comedy also; the one would make its personages worse, and the other better, than the men of the present day.

3. A THIRD difference in these arts is in the manner in which each kind of object is represented. Given both the same means and the same kind of object for imitation, one may either (1) speak at one moment in narrative and at another in an assumed character, as Homer does; or (2) one may remain the same throughout, without any such change; or (3) the imitators may represent the whole story dramatically, as though they were actually doing the things described.

---

[1] Cleophon wrote a sort of epic of everyday life (cf. the allusion to his diction in Chap. 22); Hegemon wrote parodies of Epic in the same style as *The Battle of Frogs and Mice*, and so presumably did Nicochares, of whom nothing else is known. The Greek word 'deilos' means 'cowardly', so *Deiliad* suggests an epic of cowardice, the 'Poltrooniad', cf. Pope's *Dunciad*.   [2] See p. 3 n. 1 and p. 5 n. 2.

[3] Argas wrote nomes in the style of parody or satire. The gap in the text should probably be filled with the name of a writer of serious nomes. Timotheus and Philoxenus both wrote dithyrambs on the story of Polyphemus, the Cyclops, and as there is evidence that Philoxenus' treatment was satyric, we may assume that Timotheus treated his theme seriously and 'idealized' Polyphemus.

As we said at the beginning, therefore, the differences in the imitation of these arts come under three heads, their means, their objects, and their manner.

So that as an imitator Sophocles will be on one side akin to Homer, both portraying good men; and on another to Aristophanes, since both present their personages as acting and doing. This in fact, according to some, is the reason for plays being termed dramas, because in a play the personages act the story. Hence too both Tragedy and Comedy are claimed by the Dorians as their discoveries; Comedy by the Megarians—by those in Greece as having arisen when Megara became a democracy,[1] and by the Sicilian Megarians[2] on the ground that the poet Epicharmus[3] was of their country, and a good deal earlier than Chionides and Magnes;[3] even Tragedy also is claimed by certain of the Peloponnesian Dorians.[4] In support of this claim they point to the words 'comedy' and 'drama'. Their word for the outlying hamlets, they say, is *comae*, whereas Athenians call them *demes*—thus assuming that comedians got the name not from their *comoe* or revels, but from their strolling from hamlet to hamlet, lack of appreciation keeping them

[1] About 600 B.C. when the 'tyrant', Theagenes, was expelled.

[2] i.e. in Megara Hyblaea.

[3] Epicharmus and Phormis were credited with the origin of the Comedy of Manners in which types of 'ordinary people' were depicted, as in the New Comedy which developed after the loss of Athenian independence at the battle of Chaeronea in 338 B.C., and was influenced by Aristotle's theory of drama. Epicharmus was probably writing Sicilian comedies before the beginning of the fifth century; Chionides and Magnes, whom Aristotle seems to regard as the earliest comic poets of Athens, wrote in the first half of the fifth century.

[4] Especially the people of Sicyon.

out of the city. Their word also for 'to act', they say, is *dran*, whereas Athenians use *prattein*.[1]

So much, then, as to the number and nature of the points of difference in the imitation of these arts.

4–5. Aristotle finds the origin of poetry, or more strictly of dramatic poetry, to which he now begins to confine his attention, in two human instincts, or rather in three, for after specifying 'two causes, each of them part of human nature', at the end of the paragraph he adds a third. The three are (1) the artist's instinct for imitation, (2) our instinctive pleasure in recognizing a good imitation, (3) our instinctive pleasure in harmony and rhythm.

He next traces the gradual evolution of tragedy out of laudatory hymns to the gods, through the 'heroic' stage (Iliad and Odyssey) to the preludes improvised by the leaders of a Dithyrambic chorus to state the theme or introduce their song, and thence by gradual stages to the serious dignity of what we know as Greek Tragedy. Comedy he derives from similar improvisations of a scurrilous character spoken by the leader, who was probably also the author, of a phallus-song, a ribald hymn in honour of Phales, god of fertility and companion of Dionysus. There is an example of this ritual in Aristophanes' Acharnians (l. 241 et seq.) where Dicaeopolis improvises speeches to introduce the phallus-song (ll. 263–79). Aristotle notes that 'Homer'

1 The claim of the Dorians is based on the theory that the word 'drama' is derived from the Dorian word for 'doing' or 'acting' and that 'comedy' comes from the Dorian word for the villages in which strolling players gave their primitive 'comic' performances. Aristotle does not seem to endorse either claim. For a full treatment of the origins of tragedy and comedy the reader should consult, e.g., Haigh's *The Tragic Drama of the Greeks* and *The Attic Theatre*, both published by the Clarendon Press; Cornford's *The Origin of Comedy* (Arnold), and Norwood's *Greek Comedy* (Methuen).

supplies a sort of additional parentage, since in his 'comic'
Margites (*a mock-heroic story of a rich fool who 'knew*
many works but knew them all ill'), as in his epics, he was
the first to dramatize and to 'generalize' his themes instead
of praising or parodying real individuals. At the end of
Chapter 5 he distinguishes the characteristics of Epic and
of Tragedy. This process of comparison is continued in
Chapters 23, 24, and 26.

4. It is clear that the general origin of poetry was due
to two causes, each of them part of human nature.
Imitation is natural to man from childhood, one of his
advantages over the lower animals being this, that he
is the most imitative creature in the world, and learns
at first by imitation. And it is also natural for all to
delight in works of imitation. The truth of this second
point is shown by experience: though the objects
themselves may be painful to see, we delight to view
the most realistic representations of them in art, the
forms for example of the lowest animals and of dead
bodies.[1] The explanation is to be found in a further
fact: to be learning something is the greatest of plea-
sures not only to the philosopher but also to the rest
of mankind, however small their capacity for it; the
reason of the delight in seeing pictures is that one
is at the same time learning—gathering the meaning
of things, e.g. that the man there is so-and-so; for if
one has not seen the thing before, one's pleasure will
not be in the picture as an imitation of it, but will be
due to the execution or colouring or some similar
cause. Imitation, then, being natural to us—as also

[1] Rembrandt's *Lesson in Anatomy* is a good example.

the sense of harmony and rhythm, the metres being obviously species of rhythms[1]—it was through their original aptitude, and by a series of improvements for the most part gradual on their first efforts, that they created poetry out of their improvisations.

Poetry, however, soon broke up into two kinds according to the differences of character in the individual poets; for the graver among them would represent noble actions, and those of noble personages; and the meaner sort the actions of the ignoble. The latter class produced invectives at first, just as others did hymns and panegyrics. We know of no such poem by any of the pre-Homeric poets, though there were probably many such writers among them; instances, however, may be found from Homer downwards, e.g. his *Margites*,[2] and the similar poems of others. In this poetry of invective its natural fitness brought an iambic metre into use; hence our present term 'iambic', because it was the metre of their 'iambs' or invectives against one another. The result was that the old poets became some of them writers of heroic and others of iambic verse. Homer's position, however, is peculiar: just as he was in the serious style the poet of poets, standing alone not only through the literary excellence, but also through the dramatic character of his imitations, so too he was the first to outline for us the general forms of Comedy by producing not a dramatic

---

[1] Darwin says that 'the perception, if not the enjoyment, of musical cadences and of rhythm is probably common to all animals'. Certainly for human beings there is a natural affinity between emotion and rhythm.

A rhythm runs on without regular breaks, e.g. the dactylic rhythm of the blacksmith's hammer or the trotting horse. A metre is a *species* of rhythm, i.e. one broken up into a regular pattern.

[2] See Introduction to these chapters (p. 9).

invective, but a dramatic picture of the Ridiculous; his *Margites* in fact stands in the same relation to our comedies as the *Iliad* and *Odyssey* to our tragedies. As soon, however, as Tragedy and Comedy appeared in the field, those naturally drawn to the one line of poetry became writers of comedies instead of iambs, and those naturally drawn to the other, writers of tragedies instead of epics, because these new modes of art were grander and of more esteem than the old.

If it be asked whether Tragedy is now fully developed in its formative elements,[1] to consider that, and decide it theoretically and in relation to the stage is a matter for another inquiry.

It certainly began in improvisations—as did also Comedy; the one originating with the prelude to the Dithyramb,[2] the other with the prelude to the phallic songs, which still survive as institutions in many of our cities.   And its advance after that was little by little, through their improving on whatever they had before them at each stage.   It was in fact only after a long series of changes that the movement of Tragedy stopped on its attaining to its natural form.[2]   (1) The number of actors was first increased to two by Aeschylus,[3] who curtailed the business of the Chorus, and made the dialogue, or spoken portion, take the lead-

---

[1] It is Aristotle's theory that living things develop until they have achieved the form natural to them. He assumes that Tragedy has thus achieved its 'form', but declines to consider whether any further development is possible in the various constituent elements of tragedy i.e. plot, character, diction, thought, spectacle, and melody (See Chapter 6, p. 17).

[2] See Chapter 1, p. 3, n. 1, and for 'phallic songs' see Introduction to Chapters 4 and 5. The leader started the chorus by improvising a prelude.

[3] Each actor could play more than one part.

ing part in the play. (2) A third actor and scenery were due to Sophocles. (3) Tragedy acquired also its magnitude.[1] Discarding short stories and a ludicrous diction, through its passing out of its satyric stage,[2] it assumed, though only at a late point in its progress, a tone of dignity; and its metre changed then from trochaic to iambic. The reason for their original use of the trochaic tetrameter was that their poetry was satyric and more connected with dancing than it now is. As soon, however, as a spoken part came in, nature herself found the appropriate metre. The iambic, we know, is the most speakable of metres, as is shown by the fact that we very often fall into it in conversation,[3] whereas we rarely talk hexameters, and only when we depart from the speaking tone of voice. (4) Another change was a plurality of episodes or acts. As for the remaining matters, the superadded embellishments[4] and the account of their introduction, these must be taken as said, as it would probably be a long piece of work to go through the details.

[1] The word implies both length and dignity.

[2] It is clearly Aristotle's opinion, though he does not definitely state it, that an early stage in the evolution of Tragedy was the Satyr play, a brief and jocular interlude, the performers in which appeared as Dionysus' goat-footed followers. Hence the name, *tragos* being the Greek for a goat. None of these primitive Satyr plays survive. Later at the Athenian festivals each competitor produced a trilogy, i.e. a group of three tragedies, and a comic Satyr play. We have fragments of one by Sophocles (*The Trackers*), and from the *Cyclops* of Euripides get an even better idea of what a Satyr play was like in the 5th century, B.C.

As there was a lot of dancing in it, the metre used was the trochaic tetrameter, e.g. Ín the spríng a yoúng man's fáncy líghtly túrns to thoúghts of lóve.

The origin of tragedy is obscure, but on the whole the available evidence tells against Aristotle's theory.

[3] It is the same in English with blank verse.

[4] i.e. costumes, masks, &c.

5. As for Comedy, it is (as has been observed) an imitation of men worse than the average; worse, however, not as regards any and every sort of fault, but only as regards one particular kind, the Ridiculous, which is a species of the Ugly.[1] The Ridiculous may be defined as a blunder or deformity not productive of pain or harm to others; the mask, for instance, that excites laughter, is something ugly and distorted without causing pain.

Though the successive changes in Tragedy and their authors are not unknown, we cannot say the same of Comedy; its early stages passed unnoticed, because it was not as yet taken up in a serious way. It was only at a late point in its progress that a chorus of comedians was officially granted by the archon; they used to be mere volunteers. It had also already certain definite forms at the time when the record of those termed comic poets begins. Who it was who supplied it with masks, or prologues, or a plurality of actors and the like, has remained unknown. The invented Fable, or Plot, however, originated in Sicily, with Epicharmus and Phormis;[2] of Athenian poets Crates[3] was the first to drop the Comedy of invective and frame stories of

[1] To a Greek 'ugly' was the equivalent of 'bad'. However, the characters of Comedy have only one of the many qualities which make up Ugliness or Badness. They are not harmful, but they *are* ridiculous and therefore contemptible.

Aristotle obviously has in mind the farcical comedies of his own day, but his view is applicable also to the 'thoughtful laughter' of more serious comedy. The comic, like the tragic, dramatist gives a picture and therefore necessarily a criticism of human life, but the emotion he conveys is not 'the pity of it!', but 'what fools these mortals be!'.

[2] See Chapter 3, p. 7, n. 3.

[3] He won his first victory in 449. Some fragments of his comedies survive.

a general and non-personal nature, in other words, Fables or Plots.

Epic poetry, then, has been seen to agree with Tragedy to this extent, in that it is an imitation of serious subjects in a grand kind of verse. It differs from it, however, (1) in that it is in one kind of verse and in narrative form; and (2) in its length—which is due to its action having no fixed limit of time, whereas Tragedy endeavours to keep as far as possible within a single circuit of the sun, or something near that.[1] This, I say, is another point of difference between them, though at first the practice in this respect was just the same in tragedies as in epic poems. They differ also (3) in their constituents, some being common to both and others peculiar to Tragedy—hence a judge of good and bad in Tragedy is a judge of that in epic poetry also. All the parts of an epic are included in Tragedy; but those of Tragedy are not all of them to be found in the Epic.[2]

6. *This chapter is the core of the* Poetics. *In his famous definition of tragedy Aristotle resumes what has been said already and devotes almost all the following chapters to explaining it further. Having shown that the arts differ one from another in the objects 'imitated', in the means employed, and in the mode of imitation, Aristotle now shows (1) that the 'object imitated' by tragedy is an action or piece of life of serious interest, complete in itself and*

[1] The rigid 'dramatic unities' find no authority in the *Poetics*. Aristotle states here not a rule but a general practice. He is equally vague about 'unity of place' in Chapter 24. The only unity on which he insists is the 'unity of subject'; a play must not be an 'omnibus' of plots but a single story. See Introduction pp. xxi–xxiv.

[2] Of the 'parts' of tragedy (see Chapter 6, p. 17) plot, character, diction and thought are parts also of Epic, but not spectacle and melody.

'having magnitude', i.e. long enough and serious enough to be more than trivial; (2) that the means employed is language 'flavoured' by all the available 'sauces', such as melody and poetic diction; and (3) that the mode of imitation is dramatic, i.e. the story is told not by narration but by persons acting in character who excite in the auditors pity and fear, and by providing an outlet for these and similar emotions produce a sense of pleasurable relief.

Plato, who was more emotional than Aristotle, held that the effect of art on human nature might be a dangerous incontinence of emotion through the deliberate cultivation of violent feelings which ought in the interest of public morality to be discouraged. That, at least, is one of Plato's views on Art. Aristotle, realizing the risks of inhibition, replies that this effect is not only pleasurable but also beneficial. Tragedy is a sort of nervous specific which provides a 'Catharsis'—we might say 'a good clearance' —of emotions which might otherwise break out inconveniently. It saves us from psychical distress by providing an emotional outlet.

A paraphrase of a passage in Plato's Laws may help to explain this view. 'When babies are restless, you don't prescribe quiet for them; you sing to them and rock them to and fro. When Bacchants are restless and frenzied, they cure themselves by singing and dancing. In both cases the external agitation, getting the better of the internal agitation, produces peace and calm. The baby goes to sleep: the Bacchant returns to a sound mind.' That agrees with Aristotle's view. The excitement of tragedy provides for our feelings a pleasurable relief. A 'good cry' acts as an emotional aperient. We feel all the better for it and leave the theatre 'in peace of mind, all passion spent'.

Tragedy is then analysed into six constituent elements.

Of these, three are the objects imitated, (1) a plot or piece of life (human actions or experiences); (2) the characters of the personae *(moral qualities); (3) the thoughts which they express (intellectual qualities). Two of the elements, diction and melody, are the means of imitation employed. The sixth, 'spectacle', is the mode of imitation, by which the story is presented on a stage before an audience.*

Of these constituent parts Aristotle regards the Plot as by far the most important—'the life and soul of tragedy'. No amount of psychological ingenuity in drawing character, no degree of poetic or rhetorical brilliance can make a tragedy, because it is in essence a story. *In the same way you can have no picture without some sort of shape or design. Through the whole of the* Poetics *runs this insistence on the primary importance of plot, which is the main subject of discussion—with one irrelevant digression—up to the end of Chapter* 18.

6. RESERVING hexameter poetry[1] and Comedy for consideration hereafter, let us proceed now to the discussion of Tragedy; before doing so, however, we must gather up the definition resulting from what has been said. A tragedy, then, is the imitation of an action that is serious, has magnitude, and is complete in itself; in language with pleasurable accessories,[2] each kind brought in separately in the various parts of the work; in a dramatic, not in a narrative form; with incidents arousing pity and fear, wherewith to accomplish its catharsis of such emotions. Here by 'language with

[1] Hexameter poetry, i.e. epic, is discussed in Chapters 23, 24, and 26. Comedy he forgot to discuss further, or perhaps his discussion of it is lost.

[2] These are the various metres and the musical accompaniment used in the different parts of the play. Aristotle regards them as a kind of ornament or sauce to the main dish.

pleasurable accessories' I mean that with rhythm and
harmony or song superadded; and by 'the kinds separately' I mean that some portions are worked out with
verse only, and others in turn with song.

I. As they act the stories, it follows that in the first
place the Spectacle (or stage-appearance of the actors)
must be some part of the whole; and in the second place
Melody and Diction, these two being the means of
their imitation. Here by 'Diction' I mean merely this,
the composition of the verses; and by 'Melody', what
is too completely understood to require explanation.
But further: the subject represented also is an action;
and the action involves agents, who must necessarily
have their distinctive qualities both of character and
thought, since it is from these that we ascribe certain
qualities to their actions. There are in the natural
order of things, therefore, two causes—Character and
Thought—of their actions, and consequently of their
success or failure in their lives. Now the action (that
which is done) is represented in the play by the Fable
or Plot. The Plot, in our present sense of the term,
is simply this, the combination of the incidents or
things done in the story; whereas Character is what
makes us ascribe certain moral qualities to the agents;
and Thought is shown in all they say when proving
a particular point or, it may be, enunciating a general
truth. There are six parts consequently of every
tragedy, which determine its quality, viz. Plot,
Character, Diction, Thought, Spectacle, and Melody;
two of them arising from the means, one from the
manner, and three from the objects of the dramatic
imitation; and there is nothing else besides these
six. Of these elements, then, practically all of the

dramatists have made due use, as all plays alike admit of Spectacle, Character, Plot, Diction, Melody, and Thought.

II. The most important of the six is the combination of the incidents of the story. Tragedy is essentially an imitation not of persons but of action and life, of happiness and misery. All human happiness or misery takes the form of action; the end aimed at is a certain kind of activity, not a quality.[1] Character gives us qualities, but it is in our actions—what we do—that we are happy or the reverse. In a play accordingly they do not act in order to portray the Characters; they include the Characters for the sake of the action. So that it is the action in it, i.e. its Fable or Plot, that is the end and purpose of the tragedy; and the end is everywhere the chief thing. Besides this, a tragedy is impossible without action, but there may be one without Character. The tragedies of most of the moderns are characterless—a defect common among poets of all kinds, and with its counterpart in painting in Zeuxis as compared with Polygnotus;[2] for whereas the latter is strong in character, the work of Zeuxis is devoid of it. And again: one may string together a series of characteristic speeches of the

[1] The 'end' at which the dramatist aims is the representation not of qualities of character but of *action*, a piece of life presented in a story. Psychological analysis adds much to the interest of a play or a novel, but a plot or story is the one essential without which there can be neither play nor novel.

[2] Zeuxis is mentioned again in Chapter 25 as a painter of 'idealized' portraits. Apparently they were beautiful without expressing the character of the sitter. Polygnotus is mentioned in Chapter 2 as a painter whose 'personages are better than we are'. He could 'ennoble' his sitters and yet express their character. So could Raeburn. Lawrence might serve as a parallel to Zeuxis.

utmost finish as regards Diction and Thought, and yet fail to produce the true tragic effect; but one will have much better success with a tragedy which, however inferior in these respects, has a Plot, a combination of incidents, in it. And again: the most powerful elements of attraction in Tragedy, the Peripeties and Discoveries,[1] are parts of the Plot. A further proof is in the fact that beginners succeed earlier with the Diction and Characters than with the construction of a story; and the same may be said of nearly all the early dramatists. We maintain, therefore, that the first essential, the life and soul, so to speak, of Tragedy is the Plot; and that the Characters come second—compare the parallel in painting, where the most beautiful colours laid on without order will not give one the same pleasure as a simple black-and-white sketch of a portrait.[2] We maintain that Tragedy is primarily an imitation of action, and that it is mainly for the sake of the action that it imitates the personal agents. Third comes the element of Thought, i.e. the power of saying whatever can be said, or what is appropriate to the occasion. This is what, in the speeches in Tragedy, falls under the arts of Politics and Rhetoric;[3] for the older poets make their personages discourse like statesmen, and the moderns like rhetoricians. One must not confuse it with Character. Character in a

---

[1] These are explained and discussed in Chapters 11 and 16.

[2] i.e. the plot is to the drama what the design or composition is to the picture. There must in both cases be selection.

[3] This is explained more fully in Chapter 19. 'Thought', in the sense of the Greek word which Aristotle uses, means all that is expressed or effected by the use of words. 'What to say in every case' is the subject-matter of the art of Rhetoric—and of Politics too in a time when speech-making was the sole instrument of persuasion.

play is that which reveals the moral purpose of the agents,[1] i.e. the sort of thing they seek or avoid, where that is not obvious—hence there is no room for Character in a speech on a purely indifferent subject. Thought, on the other hand, is shown in all they say when proving or disproving some particular point, or enunciating some universal proposition. Fourth among the literary elements is the Diction of the personages, i.e. as before explained, the expression of their thoughts in words, which is practically the same thing with verse as with prose. As for the two remaining parts, the Melody is the greatest of the pleasurable accessories of Tragedy. The Spectacle, though an attraction, is the least artistic of all the parts, and has least to do with the art of poetry. The tragic effect is quite possible without a public performance and actors; and besides, the getting-up of the Spectacle is more a matter for the costumier than the poet.

7. *In the definition of tragedy at the beginning of Chapter 6 the action represented in tragedy must 'have magnitude'. This chapter discusses the question of 'magnitude', i.e. the proper length of a tragic play. It must be a whole story, not a collection of incidents. And if that whole is to be beautiful, it must be long enough to allow us to appreciate the orderly arrangement of the parts, i.e. the development from an incident, which may reasonably be detached from its antecedent causes and taken as a 'beginning', through the intermediate stages to an end that is inevitable or*

[1] i.e. their Will, which can best be revealed by placing a character in a position in which the choice of alternative actions is not easy or obvious. A man who chooses, e.g., vengeance rather than safety reveals his character by his exercise of Will. A man who at dinner chooses grouse rather than rabbit reveals nothing, because no sane man would choose otherwise.

at any rate probable. On the other hand, it must not— like some Chinese plays—be so long that the beginning is forgotten before the end is reached. Similarly, according to this view an animal so minute that the proportion of parts to whole cannot be distinguished is not beautiful— except under a microscope. Nor would an animal a thousand miles long be beautiful, because—even in a racing motor—we could get no impression of it as a whole. Beauty consists in a proper relation between the whole and its parts. Provided that a play is thus 'well-proportioned' and can be readily comprehended as a whole, then the bigger the better. In any case it must be long enough to allow room for the sequence of events by which the hero falls from happiness into misfortune.

7. Having thus distinguished the parts, let us now consider the proper construction of the Fable or Plot, as that is at once the first and the most important thing in Tragedy. We have laid it down that a tragedy is an imitation of an action that is whole and complete in itself and of some magnitude; for a whole may be of no magnitude to speak of. Now a whole is that which has beginning, middle, and end. A beginning is that which is not itself necessarily after anything else, and which has naturally something else after it; an end is that which is naturally after something itself, either as its necessary or usual consequent, and with nothing else after it; and a middle, that which is by nature after one thing and has also another after it. A well-constructed Plot, therefore, cannot either begin or end at any point one likes; beginning and end in it must be of the kind just described. Again: to be beautiful, a living creature, and every whole made up

of parts, must not only present a certain order in its arrangement of parts, but also be of a certain definite magnitude. Beauty is a matter of size and order, and therefore impossible either (1) in a very minute creature, since our perception becomes indistinct as it approaches instantaneity;[1] or (2) in a creature of vast size—one, say, 1,000 miles long—as in that case, instead of the object being seen all at once, the unity or wholeness of it is lost to the beholder. Just in the same way, then, as a beautiful whole made up of parts, or a beautiful living creature, must be of some size, and of a size to be taken in by the eye, so a story or Plot must be of some length, but of a length to be taken in by the memory. As for the limit of its length, so far as that is relative to public performances and spectators, it does not fall within the theory of poetry.[2] If they had to perform a hundred tragedies, they would be timed by water-clocks, as they are said to have been at one period.[3] The limit, however, set by the actual nature of the thing is this: the longer the story, consistently with its being comprehensible as a whole, the finer it is by reason of its magnitude. As a rough general formula, 'a length which allows of the hero passing by a series of probable or necessary stages from misfortune to happiness, or from happiness to

[1] i.e. so that we cannot distinguish the parts and therefore get no sense of proportion.

[2] The proper length of a play may be dictated by the number of plays to be presented at a religious festival (e.g. three tragedies and a satyr play) or in modern days at a drama festival. But that practical limit has nothing to do with the theoretical limit, i.e. the limit proper to a play as such.

[3] The words are doubtful. There is no evidence that the performance of plays was ever regulated by a water-clock, the Greek equivalent of our hour-glass. In the law-courts speeches were thus limited and the allusion may be to that practice.

misfortune', may suffice as a limit for the magnitude of the story.

8–9. *These chapters elaborate the words 'complete in itself' in the definition of tragedy at the beginning of Chapter 6. The plot or story must have unity of form, it must be a single whole. The story of a single hero's life does not necessarily have formal unity. The incidents selected for the plot of a drama must be such that each leads on to the next, so that they form a coherent whole, such that the removal or transposition of any incident would destroy the coherence. This unity of form is attained by making the content of the story 'universal'. An annalist— Aristotle apparently has no conception of what we call philosophic history—recounts actual events chronologically without showing the nexus of cause and effect. History, in this sense, merely tells us what did happen; tragedy shows us what could, or indeed must, happen. The poet, whether in epic or in drama, shows us what persons of a certain type inevitably or probably do and say and suffer. The truth he tells is of universal application, even though he is telling the story of events which actually happened to real people, for even so he is the 'maker' of the story, because he so selects the incidents as to show how and why they occurred. It is this inevitable sequence of cause and effect which arouses the emotions proper to tragedy. A mere accident does not arouse so much fear and pity as a disaster which we see to be inevitable in the sequence of events.*

There is thus in the nature of tragic art no reason why the poet should not invent both names and incidents. The reason why this was so seldom done in Greek tragedy is to be found in its religious origin. Its original object was to retell the old sagas in a new form and with new meaning.

*It was this which limited the choice of plots. Aristotle,
however, makes no allusion to this historical fact. Tragedians, he says, need not rigidly and in detail adhere to
the traditional stories but are well advised to keep the
historic—or, as we should say, mythical—names, because
that helps, as Pooh Bah says, 'to give artistic verisimilitude to a bald and unconvincing narrative'. 'What
has happened is manifestly possible, else it would not have
come to pass.' (See p. 26).*

8. THE Unity of a Plot does not consist, as some suppose, in its having one man as its subject. An infinity
of things befall that one man, some of which it is impossible to reduce to unity; and in like manner there
are many actions of one man which cannot be made
to form one action. One sees, therefore, the mistake
of all the poets who have written a *Heracleid*, a *Theseid*,
or similar poems; they suppose that, because Heracles
was one man, the story also of Heracles must be one
story.[1] Homer, however, evidently understood this
point quite well, whether by art or instinct, just in the
same way as he excels the rest in every other respect.
In writing an *Odyssey*, he did not make the poem cover
all that ever befell his hero—it befell him, for instance,
to get wounded on Parnassus and also to feign madness at the time of the call to arms, but the two incidents had no probable or necessary connexion with
one another—instead of doing that, he took an action
with a Unity of the kind we are describing as the subject of the *Odyssey*,[2] as also of the *Iliad*. The truth is
that, just as in the other imitative arts one imitation

---

[1] Their only claim to unity is that they have a single hero.
[2] See the end of Chapter 17, p. 49.

is always of one thing, so in poetry the story, as an imitation of action, must represent one action, a complete whole, with its several incidents so closely connected that the transposal or withdrawal of any one of them will disjoin and dislocate the whole. For that which makes no perceptible difference by its presence or absence is no real part of the whole.

9. FROM what we have said it will be seen that the poet's function is to describe, not the thing that has happened, but the kind of thing that might happen, i.e. what is possible as being probable or necessary. The distinction between historian and poet is not in the one writing prose and the other verse—you might put the work of Herodotus into verse and it would still be a species of history; it consists really in this, that the one describes the thing that has been, and the other a kind of thing that might be. Hence poetry is something more philosophic[1] and of graver import than history, since its statements are of the nature rather of universals, whereas those of history are singulars. By a universal statement[2] I mean a statement of what such or such a kind of man will probably or necessarily say or do—which is the aim of poetry, though it affixes proper names to the characters; by a singular statement I mean a statement of what, say, Alcibiades did or had done to him. In Comedy this has become clear by this time; it is only when their plot is already made up of probable incidents that they

---

[1] We might with equal truth say 'scientific', since tragedy, like science, induces general truths ('universals') from particular facts ('singulars'). Unlike the annalist, the poet needs a knowledge of life and a grasp of general principles. He presents to us the immutable characteristics of human nature.   [2] Or 'general truth'.

give it a basis of proper names, choosing for the purpose any names that may occur to them, instead of
writing like the old iambic poets about particular persons.[1] In Tragedy, however, they still adhere to the
historic names; and for this reason: what convinces is
the possible; now whereas we are not yet sure as to
the possibility of that which has not happened, that
which has happened is manifestly possible, else it
would not have come to pass. Nevertheless even in
Tragedy there are some plays with but one or two
known names in them, the rest being inventions; and
there are some without a single known name, e.g.
Agathon's *Antheus*,[2] in which both incidents and
names are of the poet's invention; and it is no less
delightful on that account. So that one must not aim
at a rigid adherence to the traditional stories on which
tragedies are based. It would be absurd, in fact, to do
so, as even the known stories are only known to a few,
though they are a delight none the less to all.

It is evident from the above that the poet must be
more the poet[3] of his stories or Plots than of his verses,
inasmuch as he is a poet by virtue of the imitative
element in his work, and it is actions that he imitates.
And if he should come to take a subject from actual

[1] Many of Aristophanes' characters are real people, but in later Greek
Comedy the names indicate types. This is true also of Tragedy, since in
the traditional stories, although the *personae* are supposed to be 'real
people', each character has become a type. In Chapter 17 the tragedian
is advised to sketch in outline a coherent plot before inserting the
names and episodes.

[2] Agathon was Euripides' most successful rival. The scene of Plato's
Symposium is the banquet in honour of the victory of one of his tragedies
in 416 B.C. Evidently the story of his *Antheus* was not traditional, but
invented, so that it forms a link between late Athenian Tragedy and the
Middle and New Comedy.   [3] i.e. 'maker'.

history, he is none the less a poet for that; since some historic occurrences may very well be in the probable and possible order of things; and it is in virtue of *that* that he is their poet.[1]

Of simple[2] Plots and actions the episodic are the worst. I call a Plot episodic when there is neither probability nor necessity in the sequence of its episodes. Actions of this sort bad poets construct through their own fault, and good ones on account of the players.[3] His work being for public performance, a good poet often stretches out a Plot beyond its capacity, and is thus obliged to twist the sequence of incident.

Tragedy, however, is an imitation not only of a complete action, but also of incidents arousing pity and fear. Such incidents have the very greatest effect on the mind when they occur unexpectedly and at the same time in consequence of one another; there is then more of the marvellous in them than if they happened of themselves or by mere chance. Even matters of chance seem most marvellous if there is some appearance of design in them; as for instance the statue of Mitys at Argos killed the man who caused Mitys' death by falling on him when a looker-on at a public spectacle; for incidents like that we think to be

[1] Many events in history are improbable and indeed seem impossible until a poet—this includes the modern historian—'makes' the story by showing the sequence of events.

[2] 'Simple' is defined in the next chapter.

[3] Cf. Sheridan's *The Critic*, Act II:

Under Prompter. Sir, the Carpenter says it is impossible you can go to the Park Scene yet.

Puff. The Park Scene! No! We come first, before that, to the description scene here in the wood.

U. P. Sir, the performers have cut that out!

not without a meaning. A Plot, therefore, of this sort is necessarily finer than others.

10–12. *In the last chapter Aristotle distinguished one kind of plot as 'episodic', a sub-species of the 'simple' plot. He now explains the terms 'simple' and 'complex'. In a simple plot the hero's fortunes pass direct from happiness to misery or vice versa. In a complex plot there is a climax or turning-point at which some sort of discovery leads directly to the change of fortune, which in such a plot he calls the 'peripety', a sudden reversal of fortune's wheel. The most effective form of peripety is one that is exactly coincident with the discovery of some fact, as in the* Oedipus Tyrannus, *where Oedipus' fortune is reversed at the point where he discovers his parentage. In Sophocles'* Electra *the heroine's fortunes are changed for the better at the point at which she discovers the identity of Orestes.*

'Peripety' has often been interpreted to mean the reversal of the agent's intention, i.e. a situation in which the consequence of the hero's action is the opposite of what he intended. This boomerang device is certainly effective and full of tragic irony. It is present in the peripety of the Oedipus *and of the* Lynceus, *which Aristotle uses as illustrations. Duncan's murder in* Macbeth *is another example, since the results were not what Macbeth intended. But that is not the sense in which the word is here used.*

Discovery and peripety, as thus explained, are constituent elements of the most effective kind of tragedy. A third element, common to all tragedies, is 'suffering', i.e. the tragic incident or calamity.

Having thus distinguished what he calls 'the formative elements' in tragedy, which determine its quality, Aristotle enumerates in Chapter 12 'the separate sections'

into which it is quantitatively divided. These are all
defined in the text. Chapter 12 may be an interpolation.
At any rate at this point it seems an irrelevant digression,
which interrupts Aristotle's discursive analysis of his
definition of tragedy.

10. PLOTS are either simple or complex, since the
actions they represent are naturally of this twofold
description. The action, proceeding in the way
defined as one continuous whole I call simple, when
the change in the hero's fortunes takes place without
Peripety or Discovery; and complex, when it involves
one or the other, or both. These should each of them
arise out of the structure of the Plot itself, so as to be
the consequence, necessary or probable, of the ante-
cedents. There is a great difference between a thing
happening *propter hoc* and *post hoc*.

11. A PERIPETY is the change of the kind described[1]
from one state of things within the play to its opposite,
and that too in the way we are saying, in the probable
or necessary sequence of events; as it is for instance in
Oedipus: here the opposite state of things is produced
by the Messenger, who, coming to gladden Oedipus
and to remove his fears as to his mother, reveals the
secret of his birth.[2] And in *Lynceus*: just as he is being
led off for execution, with Danaus at his side to put

[1] At the end of Chapter 7 'from misfortune to happiness or from
happiness to misfortune'.

[2] Oedipus had left Corinth to avoid fulfilling a prophecy that he would
murder his father and marry his mother. Learning of the death of King
Polybus, his supposed father, he still fears the second half of the prophecy.
The messenger assures him that Polybus and Queen Merope are not
really his parents. But this changes the whole situation by leading to the
disastrous discovery that his real parents are Laïus, whom he murdered,
and Jocasta, now his wife.

him to death, the incidents preceding this bring it about that he is saved and Danaus put to death.[1] A Discovery is, as the very word implies, a change from ignorance to knowledge, and thus to either love or hate, in the personages marked for good or evil fortune. The finest form of Discovery is one attended by Peripeties, like that which goes with the Discovery in *Oedipus*. There are no doubt other forms of it; what we have said may happen in a way in reference to inanimate things, even things of a very casual kind; and it is also possible to discover whether someone has done or not done something. But the form most directly connected with the Plot and the action of the piece is the first-mentioned. This, with a Peripety, will arouse either pity or fear—actions of that nature being what Tragedy is assumed to represent; and it will also serve to bring about the happy or unhappy ending. The Discovery, then, being of persons, it may be that of one party only to the other, the latter being already known; or both the parties may have to discover themselves. Iphigenia, for instance, was discovered to Orestes by sending the letter; and another Discovery was required to reveal him to Iphigenia.[2]

[1] In this play by the fourth-century tragedian, Theodectes, Lynceus married Hypermnestra, who disobeyed the command of her father, Danaus, to murder him. Later, their son, Abas, fell into Danaus' hands. Danaus arraigned him on a capital charge before a tribunal, which to his surprise condemned himself. 'The dog it was that died.'

[2] In Euripides' *Iphigenia in Tauris* Orestes and his friend Pylades are about to be sacrificed to Artemis by her priestess, Iphigenia. But as they are known to be Greeks, she agrees to spare Pylades to carry a letter to her home at Argos. In case he should lose the letter, she reads it aloud and Orestes thus discovers that she is his sister. He then reveals himself to Iphigenia, giving proofs of his identity (cf. Chapters 16, p. 45, and 17, p. 48).

Two parts of the Plot, then, Peripety and Discovery, are on matters of this sort. A third part is Suffering, which we may define as an action of a destructive or painful nature, such as murders on the stage, tortures, woundings, and the like.[1] The other two have been already explained.

12. THE parts of Tragedy to be treated as formative elements in the whole were mentioned in a previous Chapter.[2] From the point of view, however, of its quantity, i.e. the separate sections into which it is divided, a tragedy has the following parts: Prologue, Episode, Exode, and a choral portion, distinguished into Parode and Stasimon; these two are common to all tragedies, whereas songs from the stage and *Commoe* are found only in some. The Prologue is all that precedes the Parode of the chorus; an Episode all that comes in between two whole choral songs; the Exode all that follows after the last choral song. In the choral portion the Parode is the whole of the first utterance of the chorus; a Stasimon, a song of the chorus without anapaests or trochees;[3] a *Commos*, a lamentation sung by chorus and actor in concert. The parts of Tragedy to be used as formative elements in the whole we have already mentioned; the above are its parts from the point of view of its quantity, or the separate sections into which it is divided.

[1] Suffering is treated in Chapters 13–14.   [2] Chapter 6, p. 17.
[3] This is not true of the Greek tragedies which have survived. In many of these the 'stasima' (i.e. the choruses sung not during entry or exit, but after the chorus have taken up their position) contain trochaic and anapaestic lines. It may, however, be true of the fourth-century tragedies with which Aristotle was familiar. That the use of the chorus had altered since the days of the three great tragedians is stated at the end of Chapter 18.

13-14. *These chapters develop Aristotle's definition of the aim of tragedy, 'to provide an outlet for such emotions as pity and fear'. This brings us to his famous description of the tragic hero, which provides the first definition of the characteristic tragic emotion as compared with what is merely horrible. This emotion—'the pity of it, Iago, the pity of it'—is not effectively aroused when a wholly good man, like Job, is brought to disaster through no fault of his own. Nor when a bad man, like Richard III, fully deserves his misfortune. The hero must be a good man and, as befits the setting of Greek tragedy, a man of high estate. As the Monk says in Chaucer's Prologue:*

> *Tragedie is to seyn a certain storie,*
> *As olde books maken us memorie,*
> *Of him that stood in greet prosperitie*
> *And is y-fallen out of heigh degree*
> *Into miserie and endeth wreccedly.*

But the Monk misses a point of great importance. The hero must not be superlatively 'virtuous and just'. There must be some error in his judgement or some flaw in his character—something wrong about him—which is the cause of his downfall. But we must never feel that he deserves it. It must be a venial error, a 'little rift within the lute'. The jealousy of Othello, Achilles' hot temper, the self-confidence of Oedipus, Macbeth's ambition are good examples.

Pity and fear may be aroused by the mere sight of disaster, what Aristotle calls 'the Spectacle', e.g. Oedipus with his eyes torn out. But the true 'proper pleasure' of tragedy, the chief end which determines its means, is independent of 'spectacle' and is felt even when the play is read without performance, because it is produced by the structure and sequence of the incidents. The most effective situation, Aristotle concludes, is where one member of a family murders—or does irreparable harm to—another member. This may be done in ignorance and the kinship be discovered afterwards, as in the story of Sohrab and Rustum. More effective still is it, if the kinship is discovered just in time to avert the doing of the deed. This rather inconsistently allows the fullest tragic effect to a play with a happy ending, which theorists of modern tragedy would not admit. But the conditions of the Greek stage could not provide a 'quick curtain'. The characters and the chorus had to achieve their exit with dignity and beauty. This necessitated some relaxation of tension after the act of murder or other disaster, and for that reason a happy ending of this sort was more appropriate than it would be on the modern stage. A modern producer of Hamlet *is apt to ring down the curtain on Horatio's speech which follows the death of Hamlet. Shakespeare, having no curtain, had to bring in Fortinbras to carry off the corpses, thus relaxing the tension before the play is over. We may also note as evidence in support of Aristotle that a sudden reprieve at the eleventh hour serves powerfully to stimulate the relief of tears.*

In Chapters 10 and 11 Aristotle distinguished three 'parts of the plot', Peripety, Discovery, and Suffering. The two former were fully discussed in Chapter 11. These chapters explain the meaning of Suffering, i.e. the kind of disaster or misfortune which is peculiarly suited to produce 'the proper pleasure of tragedy, which is the release of such emotions as pity and fear'.

13. THE next points after what we have said above will be these: (1) What is the poet to aim at, and what is he to avoid, in constructing his Plots? and

(2) What are the conditions on which the tragic effect depends?[1]

We assume that, for the finest form of Tragedy, the Plot must be not simple but complex;[2] and further, that it must imitate actions arousing pity and fear, since that is the distinctive function of this kind of imitation. It follows, therefore, that there are three forms of Plot to be avoided. (1) A good man must not be seen passing from happiness to misery, or (2) a bad man from misery to happiness. The first situation is not fear-inspiring or piteous, but simply odious to us. The second is the most untragic that can be; it has no one of the requisites of Tragedy; it does not appeal either to the human feeling[3] in us, or to our pity, or to our fears. Nor, on the other hand, should (3) an extremely bad man be seen falling from happiness into misery. Such a story may arouse the human feeling in us, but it will not move us to either pity or fear; pity is occasioned by undeserved misfortune, and fear by that of one like ourselves; so that there will be nothing either piteous or fear-inspiring in this situation. There remains, then, the intermediate kind of person, a man not pre-eminently virtuous and just, whose misfortune, however, is brought upon him not by vice and depravity but by some error of judgement,[4]

---

[1] These two points are closely connected, since the structure of the plot aims at producing the tragic effect. The treatment of the second point, the proper conditions of a 'good relief', begins at the second paragraph of Chapter 14.   [2] See Chapter 10, p. 29.

[3] i.e. our sense of 'poetic justice'.

[4] The hero must have some defect, moral or intellectual, which inevitably gives rise to some disastrous action, which is in no sense an accident yet devoid of wicked intent. The tragic hero makes a great mistake and makes it because, for all his fine qualities, he is that sort of man. Hence 'the pity of it'.

he being one of those who enjoy great reputation and prosperity; e.g. Oedipus, Thyestes, and the men of note of similar families. The perfect Plot, accordingly, must have a single, and not (as some tell us) a double issue; the change in the hero's fortunes must be not from misery to happiness, but on the contrary from happiness to misery; and the cause of it must lie not in any depravity, but in some great error on his part; the man himself being either such as we have described, or better, not worse, than that. Fact also confirms our theory. Though the poets began by accepting any tragic story that came to hand, in these days the finest tragedies are always on the story of some few families, on that of Alcmeon, Oedipus, Orestes, Meleager, Thyestes, Telephus, or any others that may have been involved, as either agents or sufferers, in some deed of horror.[1] The theoretically best tragedy, then, has a Plot of this description. The critics, therefore, are wrong who blame Euripides for taking this line in his tragedies, and giving many of them an unhappy ending. It is, as we have said, the right line to take. The best proof is this: on the stage, and in the public performances, such plays, properly worked out, are seen to be the most truly tragic; and Euripides, even if his execution be faulty in every other point,[2] is nevertheless seen to be certainly the

---

[1] Aristotle, as we have noted, omits the historical reason, that the object of Greek tragedy was to retell these stories at a religious festival.

[2] Aristotle criticizes Euripides' *Medea* (1) because Medea kills her children 'knowingly and consciously' (Chapter 14); (2) because the timely appearance of Aegeus is 'improbable' (Chapter 25); (3) because the use of the *deus ex machina* at the end depends on a stage-artifice (Chapter 15).

His other criticisms of Euripides are that his choruses are often irrelevant to the plot (Chapter 18); that in the *Iphigenia in Aulis* the heroine's

most tragic of the dramatists. After this comes the
construction of Plot which some rank first, one with a
double story (like the *Odyssey*) and an opposite issue
for the good and the bad personages.[1] It is ranked as
first only through the weakness of the audiences; the
poets merely follow their public, writing as its wishes
dictate. But the pleasure here is not that of Tragedy.
It belongs rather to Comedy, where the bitterest
enemies in the piece (e.g. Orestes and Aegisthus) walk
off good friends at the end, with no slaying of anyone
by anyone.[2]

14. THE tragic fear and pity may be aroused by the
Spectacle; but they may also be aroused by the very
structure and incidents of the play—which is the
better way and shows the better poet. The Plot in
fact should be so framed that, even without seeing the
things take place, he who simply hears the account of
them shall be filled with horror and pity at the incidents; which is just the effect that the mere recital of

character is inconsistent (Chapter 15); that in the *Orestes* the character of
Menelaus is needlessly depraved (Chapter 15); that Melanippe in the
tragedy of that title is too philosophical for a woman (Chapter 15); and
that in the *Iphigenia in Tauris* Orestes' revelation of himself is deliberate
instead of arising inevitably out of the sequence of the incidents (Chapter
16). Most modern readers feel that Euripides' plays are supremely tragic
because his characters are less heroic, more like ordinary human beings,
than those in Aeschylus and Sophocles. But this Aristotle considers a
defect. 'Tragedy is an imitation of persons better than the ordinary
man' (Chapter 15, p. 43).

[1] See the summary of the plot of the *Odyssey* at the end of Chapter 17.

[2] In Comedy, as Goethe said, 'nobody dies, everybody is married'. It
is interesting to observe that fourth-century 'tragedies' like many plays
and novels of our own time were robbed of their true tragic effect by that
'secret penchant for false sentiment' which affects both theatre-audiences
and library-subscribers. See Introduction, p. xxvi.

the story in *Oedipus* would have on one. To produce this same effect by means of the Spectacle is less artistic, and requires extraneous aid. Those, however, who make use of the Spectacle to put before us that which is merely monstrous and not productive of fear, are wholly out of touch with Tragedy;[1] not every kind of pleasure should be required of a tragedy, but only its own proper pleasure.

The tragic pleasure is that of pity and fear, and the poet has to produce it by a work of imitation; it is clear, therefore, that the causes should be included in the incidents of his story. Let us see, then, what kinds of incident strike one as horrible, or rather as piteous. In a deed of this description the parties must necessarily be either friends, or enemies, or indifferent to one another. Now when enemy does it on enemy, there is nothing to move us to pity either in his doing or in his meditating the deed, except so far as the actual pain of the sufferer is concerned; and the same is true when the parties are indifferent to one another. Whenever the tragic deed, however, is done within the family—when murder or the like is done or meditated by brother on brother,[2] by son on father,[3] by mother on son,[4] or son on mother[5]—these are the situations the poet should seek after. The traditional

---

[1] We hear in Chapter 18 of plays which relied for their effect on scenery and 'make-up', e.g. 'scenes laid in Hades'. It is, however, not the *sight* of Oedipus with his eyes torn out that gives us the emotion peculiar to tragedy, but rather the *fact* that this disaster arose inevitably from the sequence of events.

[2] e.g. Eteocles and Polyneices in the *Phoenissae*.

[3] e.g. Oedipus and Laïus in the *Oedipus Tyrannus*.

[4] e.g. Althaea and Meleager.

[5] e.g. Orestes and Clytaemnestra in Aeschylus' *Choephoroe* and in the *Electra* of Sophocles and of Euripides.

stories, accordingly, must be kept as they are, e.g. the murder of Clytaemnestra by Orestes and of Eriphyle by Alcmeon.[1] At the same time even with these there is something left to the poet himself; it is for him to devise the right way of treating them. Let us explain more clearly what we mean by 'the right way'. The deed of horror may be done by the doer knowingly and consciously, as in the old poets, and in Medea's murder of her children in Euripides. Or he may do it, but in ignorance of his relationship, and discover that afterwards, as does Oedipus in Sophocles. Here the deed is outside the play;[2] but it may be within it, like the act of Alcmeon in Astydamas,[1] or that of Telegonus in *Ulysses Wounded*.[3] A third possibility is for one meditating some deadly injury to another, in ignorance of his relationship, to make the discovery in time to draw back. These exhaust the possibilities, since the deed must necessarily be either done or not done, and either knowingly or unknowingly.[4]

[1] Alcmeon killed his mother Eriphyle because, bribed by the gift of a necklace, she had persuaded her husband Amphiaraus to go to his death in the expedition of the Seven against Thebes. The allusion here is probably to the play, mentioned a few lines later, by Astydamas, a prolific tragedian of the fourth century, who appears however to have made Alcmeon kill his mother unwittingly.

[2] Oedipus quarrelled with Laïus at a cross-road and killed him, not knowing that Laïus was his father. This occurs before the action of the play begins.

[3] Telegonus, the son of Ulysses and Circe, came to Ithaca in search of his father and killed him unwittingly. The allusion may be to a lost play by Sophocles, called *The Thorn-struck Ulysses*, which suggests a strange instrument of murder.

[4] Aristotle overlooks the fourth alternative in which A, knowing who B is, meditates but does not do the injury, e.g. Abraham and Isaac, or Hamlet finding his uncle at prayer. This is clearly not a properly tragic situation.

The worst situation is when the person is with full knowledge on the point of doing the deed, and leaves it undone. It is odious and also (through the absence of suffering) untragic; hence it is that no one is made to act thus except in some few instances, e.g. Haemon and Creon in *Antigone*.[1] Next after this comes the actual perpetration of the deed meditated. A better situation than that, however, is for the deed to be done in ignorance, and the relationship discovered afterwards, since there is nothing odious in it, and the Discovery will serve to astound us.[2] But the best of all is the last; what we have in *Cresphontes*,[3] for example, where Merope, on the point of slaying her son, recognizes him in time; in *Iphigenia*, where sister and brother are in a like position;[4] and in *Helle*, where the son recognizes his mother when on the point of giving her up to her enemy.[5]

This will explain why our tragedies are restricted (as we said just now) to such a small number of families. It was accident rather than art that led the poets in quest of subjects to embody this kind of incident in their Plots. They are still obliged,

[1] In Sophocles' play Haemon, discovered by his father Creon embracing the dead body of Antigone, draws on him, but Creon escapes.

[2] e.g. Sohrab and Rustum, or Pentheus and his mother Agave in Euripides' *Bacchae*.

[3] A lost play by Euripides. Polyphontes killed Cresphontes and took his kingdom of Messenia and his wife Merope. When her son returned later to seek vengeance, she nearly killed him but discovered in time who he was.

[4] See Chapter 11, p. 30, n. 2.

[5] The play is unknown. Nephele, divorced by her husband Athamas, sent her children Phrixus and Helle to Colchis on a ram with a golden fleece. Helle fell off and gave her name to the Hellespont. Phrixus arrived, and there begins the story of Jason's famous quest. But that does not help us here.

accordingly, to have recourse to the families in which such horrors have occurred.[1]

On the construction of the Plot, and the kind of Plot required for Tragedy, enough has now been said.

15. *This chapter deals with the delineation of character, which Aristotle regards as being, together with Peripety, Discovery, and Suffering, a part of the plot. The character delineated must be* good *of its kind. This may be a reply to Plato's criticism in the* Republic *that art is immoral because it presents 'an image of the evil' as well as of the good. But the rule probes deeper than that. Greek tragedy is on too large a scale of dignity to admit a character so mean as, e.g., Iago. According to Aristotle's view even the minor persons in a tragedy should be heroic, better than the ordinary man, and he criticizes Euripides for lowering this standard. The setting, costume, and religious occasion of Greek tragedy support this view. If a tragedian has to portray men with faults, he must, like a fashionable portrait painter, make the best of them. They must be no meaner than the plot demands. Even modern dramatists, who often take for heroes men of bad character, must show the good side of the hero's character in order to produce the tragic effect. It is the good and not the bad in the character of Orestes and of Macbeth that makes us feel their fate to be a tragedy. But in the minor characters, owing to the different circumstance of the staging, modern tragedy is not so limited.*

The other rules laid down for the delineation of character are easy to understand. It must be appropriate to the

---

[1] See Chapter 13, p. 35, n. 1, and the introduction to Chapters 8 and 9.

kind of person represented, and like the original in the saga story, e.g. Achilles in any tragedy must have high courage and a hasty temper. And the character must be consistent *throughout. Moreover, the words and actions of each person in the play must be the logical outcome of his character, just as the incidents are the logical outcome of the situation. This leads Aristotle to digress on the weakness of denouements which are not the natural outcome of the preceding incidents but arbitrarily achieved by the interference of a god or by other such mechanical devices.*

15. In the Characters there are four points to aim at. First and foremost, that they shall be good. There will be an element of character in the play, if (as has been observed)[1] what a personage says or does reveals a certain moral purpose; and a good element of character, if the purpose so revealed is good. Such goodness is possible in every type of person, even in a woman or a slave, though the one is perhaps an inferior, and the other a wholly worthless being. The second point is to make them appropriate. The Character before us may be, say, manly; but it is not appropriate in a female Character to be manly, or clever. The third is to make them like the reality, which is not the same as their being good and appropriate, in our sense of the term. The fourth is to make them consistent and the same throughout; even if the original is inconsistent and presents that type of character for the poet to imitate, he should still be consistently inconsistent. We have an instance of baseness of character, not required for the story, in Menelaus in the

[1] In Chapter 6, p. 20.

Orestes;[1] of the incongruous and unbefitting in the lamentation of Ulysses in *Scylla*,[1] and in the (clever) speech of Melanippe;[1] and of inconsistency in *Iphigenia at Aulis*, where Iphigenia[1] the suppliant is utterly unlike the later Iphigenia. The right thing, however, is in the Characters just as in the incidents of the play to endeavour always after the necessary or the probable; so that whenever such-and-such a personage says or does such-and-such a thing, it shall be the probable or necessary outcome of his character; and whenever this incident follows on that, it shall be either the necessary or the probable consequence of it. From this one sees (to digress for a moment) that the Denouement also should arise out of the plot itself, and not depend on a stage-artifice, as in *Medea*,[2] or in the story of the (arrested) departure of the Greeks in the *Iliad*.[2] Such artifice must be reserved for matters outside the play—for past events beyond human

  [1] His criticism is that Euripides did not make the best of Menelaus and thus lowered the tone of tragedy; that he put into the mouth of Melanippe philosophic reflections inappropriate to a woman (Portia is perhaps a parallel); and that the courage of the heroine at the end of the *Iphigenia in Aulis* is inconsistent with her earlier plea for mercy. (Few would endorse this.) Also that Timotheus in his dithyramb, *Scylla* (mentioned again in Chapter 26), gives Odysseus a character quite unlike that of the original, who would never have indulged in lamentation.

  [2] In *Iliad* ii the flight of the Greeks is stayed by the intervention of Athene and not as the natural result of previous incidents. In the *Medea* the entry of Aegeus is similarly 'mechanical', not caused by the sequence of events (see Chapter 25, p. 78, n. 2), and so is the spiriting away of Medea in the chariot of the Sun at the end of the play. This chariot was probably the car, or crane, which has given rise to the phrase 'the god in the car'. With a pulley attached, it was fixed to the corner of the back-scene and in it a god could be lowered or exhibited in mid air. Euripides and others used this device 'to cut the knot' instead of unravelling the plot by the logic of cause and effect. A similarly 'mechanical' device is the introduction of a god to speak a prologue describing the events antecedent to the opening of the play.

knowledge, or events yet to come, which require to be foretold or announced; since it is the privilege of the Gods to know everything. There should be nothing improbable among the actual incidents. If it be unavoidable, however, it should be outside the tragedy, like the improbability in the *Oedipus* of Sophocles.[1] But to return to the Characters. As Tragedy is an imitation of persons better than the ordinary man, we in our way should follow the example of good portrait-painters, who reproduce the distinctive features of a man, and at the same time, without losing the likeness, make him handsomer than he is. The poet in like manner, in portraying men quick or slow to anger, or with similar infirmities of character, must know how to represent them as such, and at the same time as good men, as Agathon and Homer have represented Achilles.

All these rules one must keep in mind throughout, and further, those also for such points of stage-effect as directly depend on the art of the poet,[2] since in these too one may often make mistakes. Enough, however, has been said on the subject in one of our published writings.[3]

16–18. *These three chapters form an appendix to the discussion of Plot in the preceding nine chapters. Scenes*

[1] See Chapter 14, p. 38, n. 2. It was odd that Oedipus, seeking to discover the murderer of Laïus, should not have seen a clue in the murder he had himself committed. But neither readers nor audience worry about events which take place before the opening of a play.

[2] i.e. what we call 'stage-craft', as distinct from the effects of scenery and costume.

[3] Presumably in a lost work *Of Poets*, in which Aristotle may have assembled the facts from which by induction he derived the theories here expounded. This was an 'exoteric' or popular work (cf. Introduction p. xi).

of Discovery are so important that, although already dis-
cussed in Chapters 10 *and* 11, *further instructions for*
their criticism and construction are now added in Chapter
16. *In the two following chapters Aristotle gives further*
advice for the construction of a good plot, contrasting this
with the construction of an epic poem; analyses Plot, this
time from the spectators' point of view, into Complication
and Denouement; and distinguishes four main species of
tragedy. In the first species the tragic effect is due to a
'complex' plot with a Peripety and a Discovery; in the
second to the horror of the suffering involved; in the third
to the drawing of character; in the fourth and worst to
the Spectacle. He ends the appendix with still further
insistence on the prime importance of the 'unity of subject',
the subordination of detail to the whole scheme, of which
the essential purpose is the proper emotional effect; and
adds a note on the use of the chorus, which must play its
part in the drama and not merely sing charming but
irrelevant songs.

16. DISCOVERY in general has been explained already.[1]
As for the species of Discovery, the first to be noted
is (1) the least artistic form of it, of which the poets
make most use through mere lack of invention, Discovery by signs or marks.[2] Of these signs some are
congenital, like the 'lance-head which the Earth-born
have on them', or 'stars', such as Carcinus employs

---

[1] In Chapter 11.
[2] Victorians will remember *Box and Cox*: 'Tell me, in mercy tell me,
have you a strawberry mark on your left arm?' 'No.' 'Then you are my
long-lost brother.' Here too we have birth-marks, the 'lance-head' which
marked the descendants of the Spartoi or Earth-born at Thebes, and the
'star' which the descendants of Pelops inherited as a legacy from his ivory
shoulder.

in his *Thyestes*; others acquired after birth—these latter being either marks on the body, e.g. scars, or external tokens, like necklaces, or to take another sort of instance, the ark in the Discovery in *Tyro*.[1] Even these, however, admit of two uses, a better and a worse; the scar of Ulysses is an instance; the Discovery of him through it is made in one way by the nurse and in another by the swineherds.[2] A Discovery using signs as a means of proof is less artistic, as indeed are all such. Whereas one which arises out of a scene of peripety,[3] as in the *Bath-story*, is of a better order. Next after these are (2) Discoveries made directly by the poet; which are inartistic for that very reason; e.g. Orestes' Discovery of himself in *Iphigenia*: whereas his sister reveals who she is by the letter, Orestes is made to say himself what the poet rather than the story demands.[4] This, therefore, is not far removed from the first-mentioned fault, since he might have presented certain tokens as well. Another instance is the 'shuttle's voice' in the *Tereus*

---

[1] By Sophocles. Like Moses in his cradle among the bulrushes, Tyro's twins by Poseidon were discovered in a little ark on the river Enipeus.

[2] In the Bath-story (*Od.* xix), when Odysseus arrives in disguise at his own palace, it was in accordance with the best social custom that he should be washed by the housekeeper. This was his old nurse, Eurycleia. She naturally saw the old scar on his thigh and thus recognized him. This is a good Discovery, 'arising from the incidents themselves'. To the swineherds Odysseus simply declared himself, pointing to the scar as a 'sign'. This is an inartistic Discovery, merely manufactured by the poet. Aristotle condemns as inartistic all scenes where the incidents are not the natural outcome of what has gone before.

[3] See introduction to Chapters 10–12.

[4] See Chapter 11, p. 30, n. 2. To prove to Iphigenia the truth of his story, Orestes mentions her embroidery of the Golden Fleece story and Pelops' ancient lance which was kept in her bedroom at home. This is equivalent to presenting signs or tokens.

of Sophocles.[1]   (3) A third species is Discovery
through memory, from a man's consciousness being
awakened by something seen or heard. Thus in *The
Cyprioe* of Dicaeogenes, the sight of the picture makes
the man burst into tears;[2] and in the *Tale of Alcinous*,[3]
hearing the harper Ulysses is reminded of the past
and weeps; and by this means were they discovered.
(4) A fourth kind is Discovery through reasoning;[4]
e.g. in *The Choephoroe*: 'One like me is here; there is
no one like me but Orestes; he, therefore, must be
here.' Or that which Polyidus the Sophist suggested
for *Iphigenia*;[4] since it was natural for Orestes to reflect: 'My sister was sacrificed, and I am to be sacrificed like her.' Or that in the *Tydeus* of Theodectes:
'I came to find a son, and am to die myself.' Or that
in *The Phineidae*:[5] on seeing the place the women in-
ferred their fate, that they were to die there, since there
also had they been exposed.[6]   (5) There is, too, a

---

[1] i.e. the embroidered picture by which Philomela, after her tongue
had been cut out, discovered to her sister, Procne, the story of her rape by
Tereus.

[2] Teucer in disguise was recognized in Salamis, because he burst into
tears on seeing a picture of his father, Telamon. Dicaeogenes is a fourth-
century tragedian.   [3] *Od*. viii.

[4] In these instances the discovery is either made by deductive reasoning
(e.g. Electra in the Choephoroe deduces that the lock laid on Agamemnon's tomb must be Orestes' hair) or by some one overhearing one of the
characters reasoning aloud. The examples of this method are unfortunately taken from lost plays. Polyidus apparently suggested that Orestes in
Iphigenia in Tauris, as he was led out to be sacrificed, should remark upon
the odd coincidence that the same fate should befall him and his sister, and
thus reveal his identity to his sister, Iphigenia, the priestess (cf. Chapter
17). How fortunate for Polyidus that he was not a dramatist, but a mere
critic!

[5] *Tydeus* and the *Phineidae* are lost plays of which nothing is known.
Presumably the inference was in both cases uttered aloud and this led to
discovery.   [6] Exposed to die as unwanted female babies.

composite Discovery arising from bad reasoning on the side of the other party.[1] An instance of it is in *Ulysses the False Messenger*: he said he should know the bow—which he had not seen; but to suppose from that that he would know it again (as though he had once seen it) was bad reasoning. (6) The best of all Discoveries, however, is that arising from the incidents themselves, when the great surprise comes about through a probable incident, like that in the *Oedipus* of Sophocles; and also in *Iphigenia*;[2] for it was not improbable that she should wish to have a letter taken home. These last are the only Discoveries independent of the artifices of signs and necklaces. Next after them come Discoveries through reasoning.

17. AT the time when he is constructing his Plots, and engaged on the Diction in which they are worked out, the poet should remember (1) to put the actual scenes as far as possible before his eyes. In this way, seeing everything with the vividness of an eyewitness as it were, he will devise what is appropriate, and be least likely to overlook incongruities. This is shown by what was censured in Carcinus, the return of Amphiaraus from the sanctuary; it would have passed unnoticed, if it had not been actually seen by the audience; but on the stage his play failed, the

[1] Here again the example is obscure and the play is lost. Miss Dorothy Sayers, past-mistress of the art of 'telling lies in the right way', suggests that this is the 'discovery by bluff' employed by detectives both in and out of fiction: 'This is your gun.' 'But that is not the weapon with which the murder was done.' '*How do you know that?*' An alternative interpretation is that the bad reasoning is not 'on the side of the other party', but on the side of the audience or reader. The allusion would then be to the familiar device of laying false clues.   [2] See Chapter 11, p. 30, n. 2.

incongruity of the incident offending the spectators.[1]
(2) As far as may be, too, the poet should even act his
story with the very gestures of his personages. Given
the same natural qualifications, he who feels the emotions described will be the most convincing; distress
and anger, for instance, are portrayed most truthfully
by one who is feeling them at the moment.[2] Hence
it is that poetry demands a man with a special gift
for it, or else one with a touch of madness in him; the
former can easily assume the required mood, and the
latter may be actually beside himself with emotion.
(3) His story, again, whether already made or of his
own making, he should first simplify and reduce to a
universal form, before proceeding to lengthen it out
by the insertion of episodes. The following will show
how the universal element in *Iphigenia*,[3] for instance,
may be viewed: A certain maiden having been offered
in sacrifice, and spirited away from her sacrificers into
another land, where the custom was to sacrifice all

[1] The play is lost but the point is made clear by reference to Chapter 24.
'The scene of the pursuit of Hector would be ridiculous on the stage—the
Greeks halting instead of pursuing him, and Achilles shaking his head
to stop them; but in the epic poem the absurdity is overlooked.' Similarly
a novelist who fails to 'write with his eye on the object' may sometimes
escape detection. In *The Master of Ballantrae* Stevenson describes how,
after a duel fought on ground fast-bound with frost, Mrs. Henry thrusts
the sword into the soil to clean it. On the stage the absurdity would be
immediately clear.

[2] Burke *On the Sublime and Beautiful* describes how 'the celebrated
physiognomist Campanella', who excelled as a mimic of human faces,
'composed his face, his gesture, and his whole body as nearly as he could
into the exact similitude of the person he intended to examine; and then
carefully observed what turn of mind he seemed to acquire by the change'.
He was thus able 'to enter into the dispositions and thoughts of people as
effectually as if he had been changed into the very men'. Sir Joshua
Reynolds, when painting people under the stress of emotion, adopted
a similar method.   [3] Euripides' *Iphigenia in Tauris*.

strangers to the Goddess, she was made there the
priestess of this rite. Long after that the brother of
the priestess happened to come; the fact, however, of
the oracle having for a certain reason bidden him go
thither, and his object in going, are outside the Plot
of the play. On his coming he was arrested, and about
to be sacrificed, when he revealed who he was—either
as Euripides puts it, or (as suggested by Polyidus)[1]
by the not improbable exclamation, 'So I too am
doomed to be sacrificed, as my sister was'; and the
disclosure led to his salvation. This done, the next
thing, after the proper names have been fixed as a basis
for the story, is to work in episodes or accessory incidents. One must mind, however, that the episodes
are appropriate, like Orestes' fit of madness, which
led to his arrest, and the purifying, which brought
about his salvation.[2] In plays, then, the episodes are
short; in epic poetry they serve to lengthen out the
poem. The argument of the *Odyssey* is not a long one.
A certain man has been abroad many years; Poseidon
is ever on the watch for him, and he is all alone.
Matters at home too have come to this, that his sub-
stance is being wasted and his son's death plotted by
suitors to his wife. Then he arrives there himself after
his grievous sufferings; reveals himself, and falls on
his enemies; and the end is his salvation and their
death. This being all that is proper to the *Odyssey*,
everything else in it is episode.

18. (4) THERE is a further point to be borne in mind.
Every tragedy is in part Complication and in part
Denouement; the incidents before the opening scene,

[1] Cf. Chapter 16, p. 46, n. 4.   [2] In *Iphigenia in Tauris*.

and often certain also of those within the play, forming
the Complication; and the rest the Denouement. By
Complication I mean all from the beginning of the
story to the point just before the change in the hero's
fortunes; by Denouement, all from the beginning of
the change to the end. In the *Lynceus* of Theodectes,[1]
for instance, the Complication includes, together with
the presupposed incidents, the seizure of the child and
that in turn of the parents; and the Denouement all
from the indictment for murder to the end. Now it is
right, when one speaks of a tragedy as the same or
not the same as another, to do so on the ground before
all else of their Plot, i.e. as having the same or not the
same Complication and Denouement. Yet there are
many dramatists who, after a good Complication, fail
in the Denouement. But it is necessary for both points
of construction to be always duly mastered. (5) There
are four distinct species of Tragedy—that being the
number of the constituents also that have been mentioned:[2] first, the complex Tragedy, which is all Peripety and Discovery; second, the Tragedy of suffering,
e.g. the *Ajaxes* and *Ixions*; third, the Tragedy of
character, e.g. *The Phthiotides* and *Peleus*.[3] The fourth

  [1] See Chapter 11, p. 30, n. 1. 'The child' is evidently Abas. The
point at which Complication ceases and Denouement begins is of course
arbitrary, but Aristotle is obviously right in saying that both are equally
important—modern detective stories are usually stronger in the former—
and that any play which has the same Complication and Denouement as
another is the same play, because it has the same plot.

  [2] Aristotle does not make this reference clear, but he has in his analysis
of plot already distinguished the four elements of interest by which,
according to their prominence in the play, he now classifies tragedy into
four species.

  [3] i.e. Women of Phthia (Achilles' home in Thessaly) by Sophocles;
apparently a study of feminine psychology, but unfortunately lost. Both
Sophocles and Euripides wrote a *Peleus*.

constituent is that of 'Spectacle', exemplified in *The Phorcides*, in *Prometheus*, and in all plays with the scene laid in the nether world.[1] The poet's aim, then, should be to combine every element of interest, if possible, or else the more important and the major part of them. This is now especially necessary owing to the unfair criticism to which the poet is subjected in these days. Just because there have been poets before him strong in the several species of tragedy, the critics now expect the one man to surpass that which was the strong point of each of his predecessors. (6) One should also remember what has been said more than once,[2] and not write a tragedy on an epic body of incident (i.e. one with a plurality of stories in it), by attempting to dramatize, for instance, the entire story of the *Iliad*. In the epic owing to its scale every part is treated at proper length; with a drama, however, on the same story the result is very disappointing. This is shown by the fact that all who have dramatized the fall of Ilium in its entirety, and not part by part, like Euripides, or the whole of the Niobe story,[3] instead of a portion, like Aeschylus,

[1] The effect of these plays largely depended on the 'make-up' and costume of the strange characters introduced. The daughters of Phorcys included (1) the three Graeae, witches who had one eye between them, (2) the Gorgons, (3) the Sirens, (4) the six-headed Scylla who lured sailors to death. Aeschylus gave their name to one of his satyr-plays and the *Prometheus* here mentioned is probably another. It is certainly not his tragedy, *Prometheus Bound*.

[2] e.g. in Chapter 5, p. 14 that in Epic there is no fixed limit of time-length, and earlier in this chapter that episodes serve to lengthen out an epic poem. In Chapter 23 Aristotle lays emphasis on the unity of the story in the *Iliad*, but recognizes here that such unity, owing to the length of an epic poem, is not inconsistent with a variety of incidental stories or episodes 'to relieve the uniformity of the narrative'.

[3] Niobe, the daughter of Tantalus, married Amphion, a son of Zeus,

either fail utterly or have but ill success on the stage;
for that and that alone was enough to ruin even a play
by Agathon.[1] Yet in their Peripeties, as also in their
simple plots, the poets show wonderful skill in
aiming at the kind of effect they desire—a tragic
situation and one that satisfies our human feelings, like
the clever villain (e.g. Sisyphus) deceived, or the brave
wrongdoer worsted. This is probable, however, only
in Agathon's sense, when he speaks of the probability
of even improbabilities coming to pass.[1]   (7) The
Chorus too should be regarded as one of the actors;
it should be an integral part of the whole, and take
a share in the action—such as it has in Sophocles
rather than in Euripides. With the later poets, however, the songs in a play of theirs have no more to do
with the Plot than with that of any other tragedy.
Hence it is that they are now singing mere interludes,[2] a practice first introduced by Agathon. And
yet what real difference is there between singing
such choral interludes, and attempting to fit in a

by whom she had seven sons and seven daughters. She boasted of her
superiority to the goddess Leto, who had only two children. Whereupon
Apollo, Leto's son, killed with his arrows the whole fourteen of her family.
She turned to stone, still weeping—'Niobe, all tears'. It is not known
what portion of her story Aeschylus dramatized.

[1] See Chapter 9, p. 26, n. 2. Agathon was famous for his epigrams,
e.g. the couplet here alluded to:

> This too one might call likelihood itself
> That fate unlikely should befall mankind.

Aristotle is realist enough to recognize that clever villains often escape
free. But when we see them worsted in a play, our human feelings are
satisfied and we have a delicious sense of 'poetic justice'.

[2] The word 'orchestra' (dancing ground) has long ago lost for us all
association with the dancing of the chorus, and the music played between
the acts in a modern theatre has no kind of connexion with the play.

speech, or even a whole act, from one play into another?

19, 21, 22. *In Chapter 6 Aristotle analysed tragedy into Plot, Character, Diction, Thought, Spectacle, and Melody. In all the subsequent chapters, except in Chapter 15 which deals with Character, he has been discussing the structure and the various elements of the Plot. Spectacle he deliberately omits as 'having least to do with the art of poetry' (see end of Chapter 6). Probably for the same reason he omits Melody. It remains for him to deal in Chapters 19, 21, and 22 with Thought and Diction. For the treatment of Thought, i.e. the content of the Diction, all that is expressed or effected by the use of words, we are referred to his treatise on the Art of Rhetoric, where he tells us what to say in every case. The same rules apply to the composition of an oration and of speeches in a play.*

With Diction he deals at greater length—at too great a length one might say, if Chapter 20 be included. Here it has been omitted, because it is probably an interpolation. In any case, it deals not with the use of words in poetry, but with words as such. It belongs to grammar, not to literary criticism. A similar paragraph at the end of Chapter 21 has also been omitted.

His treatment of poetic diction in Chapters 21 and 22 is fully relevant to the theme of the Poetics, *but it is indubitably disappointing. Obviously Aristotle did not appreciate poetry. But he conscientiously pins the butterfly on the board and proceeds to dissect it. Naturally the soul escapes him. But he does discover that the diction of poetry differs from the language of conversation. It must be 'clear but not mean', not utterly prosaic yet not unintelligible—two teaspoonfuls of poetry, as it were, in a wineglassful of prose—an uninspiring recipe! Yet it is as sound as scientific analysis can make it, and he does discover and stress the prime importance of the use of metaphor, though there again his explanation of metaphor may strike a modern reader as comically pedestrian. Yet it is clear, concise, and correct.*

It is true that to produce its effect poetry requires licence, but licence must be used in moderation or else the effect will be not 'poetic' but ludicrous, as happens, e.g., occasionally in the poems of Gerard Hopkins. On the other hand the 'old half-witted sheep' side of Wordsworth was the result of an endeavour to eschew poetic licence altogether.

19. THE Plot and Characters having been discussed, it remains to consider the Diction and Thought. As for the Thought, we may assume what is said of it in our Art of Rhetoric, as it belongs more properly to that department of inquiry. The Thought of the persons in a play is shown in all that must be effected by their language[1]—in every effort to prove or disprove, to arouse emotion (pity, fear, anger, and the like), or to exaggerate or minimize things. It is clear, also, that their mental procedure must be on the same lines in their actions likewise,[2] whenever they wish them to arouse pity or horror, or produce an effect of importance or probability. The only difference is that in action the effect has to be produced without explanation;[3] whereas with the spoken word it has to be

    [1] i.e. effects upon the emotions or the reason.
    [2] The Thought or Sentiments of the persons in a play may be expressed by their actions as well as by their words. The same rules for producing the desired effect apply to actions or incidents as to ideas and their expression.   [3] i.e. solely by the situation.

produced by the speaker, and result from his language. What, indeed, would be the good of the
speaker, if things appeared in the required light even
apart from anything he says?

As regards the Diction, one subject for inquiry
under this head is the turns given to the language
when spoken;[1] e.g. the difference between command
and prayer, simple statement and threat, question and
answer, and so forth. The theory of such matters,
however, belongs to Elocution and the professors of
that art. Whether the poet knows these things or not,
his art as a poet is never seriously criticized on that
account. What fault can one see in Homer's 'Sing of
the wrath, Goddess'?[2]—which Protagoras has criticized as being a command where a prayer was meant,
since to bid one do or not do, he tells us, is a command.
Let us pass over this, then, as appertaining to another
art, and not to that of poetry.[3]

21. Nouns are of two kinds, either (1) simple, i.e.
made up of non-significant parts, like the word γῆ, or
(2) double; in the latter case the word may be made
up either of a significant and a non-significant part
(a distinction which disappears in the compound), or
of two significant parts.[4] It is possible also to have

[1] i.e. the way in which the meaning is affected by the use of different
moods, tenses, &c.

[2] The opening words of the *Iliad*. Protagoras thought it improper to
dictate to a Goddess in the imperative mood.

[3] It is hard to believe that Aristotle, while very properly exhorting us
to 'pass over this', should at once proceed to perpetrate Chapter 20. So the
reader is here spared Chapter 20.

[4] e.g. (1) 'world', the parts of which have no meaning; (2) 'cur-tain';
tain is non-significant, *cur* has a meaning, but not in this compound; (3)
'tooth-brush', a compound in which both parts have their meaning.

triple, quadruple, or higher compounds, like most of our amplified names; e.g. 'Hermocaïcoxanthus'[1] and the like.

Whatever its structure, a Noun must always be either (1) the ordinary word for the thing, or (2) a strange word, or (3) a metaphor, or (4) an ornamental word,[2] or (5) a coined word, or (6) a word lengthened out, or (7) curtailed, or (8) altered in form. By the ordinary word I mean that in general use in a country; and by a strange word, one in use elsewhere. So that the same word may obviously be at once strange and ordinary, though not in reference to the same people; σίγυνος, for instance, is an ordinary word in Cyprus,[3] and a strange word with us. Metaphor consists in giving the thing a name that belongs to something else;[4] the transference being either from genus to

[1] A compound of the names of three rivers in Asia Minor, Hermus, Caicus, and Xanthus, used perhaps as the epithet of a god.

[2] This is mentioned again in Chapter 22, but its meaning is doubtful. It may refer to embellishing epithets, e.g. 'gracious' as automatically applied to royalty, or 'gallant' as used of military members of parliament.

[3] i.e. for a spear. Similarly 'ashet' is in Scotland an ordinary word for a dish, but a strange word in English ears.

[4] This account of metaphor is dry and pedantic but correct in analysis. A metaphorical statement is not literally true. But an effect of emphasis or of allusion is gained by substituting for the literally exact word a word that describes either (1) the genus of the species to which the literal word belongs—'lying at anchor' is a species of 'standing'—or (2) a species of the genus which the literal word describes—'ten thousand' is a species of large number, or (3) another species of the same genus, e.g. 'a slashing article', because invective is another species of violent assault [Aristotle's example is obscure; probably 'the bronze' is in the first case a surgeon's knife or a sword, and in the second case a cupping-bowl for bleeding: 'severing' and 'drawing off' are both species of 'taking away' or 'removing'], or (4) an analogous term, e.g. Day (A) Evening (B):: Life (C): Old Age (D). So we call Old Age the Evening of Life or Evening the Day's Old Age. All metaphors may be classed in one of these categories. But such classification is not very helpful. Aristotle remains in literary

species, or from species to genus, or from species to species, or on grounds of analogy. That from genus to species is exemplified in 'Here stands my ship'; for lying at anchor is the 'standing' of a particular kind of thing. That from species to genus in 'Truly ten thousand good deeds has Ulysses wrought', where 'ten thousand', which is a particular large number, is put in place of the generic 'a large number'. That from species to species in 'Drawing the life with the bronze', and in 'Severing with the enduring bronze'; where the poet uses 'draw' in the sense of 'sever' and 'sever' in that of 'draw', both words meaning to 'take away' something.[1] That from analogy is possible whenever there are four terms so related that the second (B) is to the first (A), as the fourth (D) to the third (C); for one may then metaphorically put B in lieu of D, and D in lieu of B. Now and then, too, they qualify the metaphor by adding on to it that to which the word it supplants is relative.[2] Thus a cup (B) is in relation to Dionysus (A) what a shield (D) is to Ares (C). The cup accordingly will be metaphorically described as the 'shield *of Dionysus*' (D+A), and the shield as the 'cup *of Ares*' (B+C). Or to take another instance: As old age (D) is to life (C), so is evening (B) to day (A). One will accordingly describe evening (B) as the 'old age *of the day*' (D+A)—or by the Empedoclean equivalent;[3] and old age (D) as the 'evening'

criticism the objective scientist, and misses the obvious point that in the use of metaphor and of all 'poetic diction' emotion is the sovereign antiseptic.

[1] See note 4 on p. 56.

[2] e.g. Flowers (A): Field (B):: Stars (C): Sky (D). We can use (D) instead of (B) and call the field a sky. The word supplanted is Field (B). Add the term to which (B) is relative, i.e., Flowers (A), and you get the metaphorical expression 'a sky of flowers'. Vice versa, you can call the sky 'a field of stars'.   [3] Unknown to us.

or 'sunset *of life*' (B+C). It may be that some of the
terms thus related have no special name of their own,
but for all that they will be metaphorically described
in just the same way. Thus to cast forth seed-corn is
called 'sowing'; but to cast forth its flame, as said of
the sun, has no special name. This nameless act (B),
however, stands in just the same relation to its object,
sunlight (A), as sowing (D) to the seed-corn (C).
Hence the expression in the poet, 'sowing around a
god-created *flame*' (D+A).[1] There is also another
form of qualified metaphor. Having given the thing
the alien name, one may by a negative addition deny
it one of the attributes naturally associated with its
new name. An instance of this would be to call the
shield not the 'cup *of Ares*', as in the former case, but
a 'cup *that holds no wine*'.[2] A coined word is a name
which, being quite unknown among a people, is given
by the poet himself; e.g. (for there are some words
that seem to be of this origin) ἔρνυγες[3] for horns, and
ἀρητήρ[4] for priest. A word is said to be lengthened out
when it has a short vowel made long, or an extra
syllable inserted; e.g. πόληος for πόλεως, Πηληιάδεω
for Πηλείδου. It is said to be curtailed when it has
lost a part;[5] e.g. κρῖ, δῶ, and ὄψ in μία γίνεται ἀμφοτέρων
ὄψ. It is an altered word when part is left as it was
and part is of the poet's making; e.g. δεξιτερόν for
δεξιόν, in δεξιτερὸν κατὰ μαζόν.

---

[1] So we say 'Hope springs eternal' where there is no literal expression
for the action of Hope.

[2] Cf. 'Drunken but not with wine' or 'Venus' bloodless war'.

[3] 'sprouters'.   [4] 'a pray-er'.

[5] English poetry enjoys similar licences, e.g. *wanwood* and *leafmeal*
(Gerard Hopkins's own invention); *wind* (lengthened); *morn* and *eve*
(curtailed); and Ezra Pound uses '*tawn*' for 'tawny'.

22. THE perfection of Diction is for it to be at once clear and not mean. The clearest indeed is that made up of the ordinary words for things, but it is mean, as is shown by the poetry of Cleophon and Sthenelus.[1] On the other hand the Diction becomes distinguished and non-prosaic by the use of unfamiliar terms, i.e. strange words, metaphors, lengthened forms, and everything that deviates from the ordinary modes of speech.—But a whole statement in such terms will be either a riddle or a barbarism, a riddle, if made up of metaphors, a barbarism, if made up of strange words. The very nature indeed of a riddle is this, to describe a fact in an impossible combination of words (which cannot be done with the real names for things, but can be with their metaphorical substitutes); e.g. 'I saw a man glue brass on another with fire', and the like.[2] The corresponding use of strange words results in a barbarism.[3]—A certain admixture, accordingly, of unfamiliar terms is necessary. These, the strange word, the metaphor, the ornamental word, &c., will save the language from seeming mean and prosaic, while the ordinary words in it will secure the requisite clearness. What helps most, however, to render the

[1] Aristophanes says that the diction of the tragic poet, Sthenelus, was unpalatable without salt and vinegar. Aristotle mentioned in Chapter 2, p. 6 that Cleophon's characters were 'on our own level'; their diction also was evidently insipid.

[2] This riddle refers to the brass cupping-bowl, which was held tight to the punctured limb and heated, so as to create a vacuum and draw blood. 'Brass' is the genus of which 'bowl' is a species; to glue and to apply are two species of the same genus. Compare Samson's riddle 'Out of the eater came forth meat, out of the strong came forth sweetness', where the riddle is made by the use of four generic instead of specific terms.

[3] Since the speech of barbarians, i.e. non-Greeks, was unintelligible, a barbarism means any unintelligible speech.

Diction at once clear and non-prosaic is the use of the lengthened, curtailed, and altered forms of words. Their deviation from the ordinary words will, by making the language unlike that in general use, give it a non-prosaic appearance; and their having much in common with the words in general use will give it the quality of clearness. It is not right, then, to condemn these modes of speech, and ridicule the poet for using them, as some have done; e.g. the elder Euclid, who said it was easy to make poetry if one were to be allowed to lengthen the words as much as one likes, and wrote a parody in this very style:—'Ἐπιχάρην εἶδον Μαραθῶνάδε βαδίζοντα, and οὐκ ἄν γ' ἐράμενος τὸν ἐκείνου ἐλλέβορον.[1] A too apparent use of these licences has certainly a ludicrous effect, but they are not alone in that; the rule of moderation applies to all the constituents of the poetic vocabulary; even with metaphors, strange words, and the rest, the effect will be the same, if one uses them improperly and with a view to provoking laughter. The proper use of them is a very different thing. To realize the difference one should take an epic verse and see how it reads when the normal words are introduced. The same should be done too with the strange word, the metaphor, and the rest; for one has only to put the ordinary words in their place to see the truth of what we are saying.

[1] The meaning of these Greek words does not matter. The point is that in epic poetry a short syllable is sometimes lengthened by accentual stress; 'The elder Euclid' (unknown) seems to have written a parody in which an excessive use of this licence produced an intentionally ludicrous effect. Stephen Phillips, a late-Victorian poet, using a similar licence wrote in a blank-verse poem, 'Agámemnón bowed óver ánd from his whéel', which moved a parodist in *Punch* to write 'with a view to provoking laughter': 'She á millíner wás and hér brothérs Dynámitérs'.

The same iambic, for instance, is found in Aeschylus and Euripides, and as it stands in the former it is a poor line; whereas Euripides, by the change of a single word, the substitution of a strange for what is by usage the ordinary word, has made it seem a fine one. Aeschylus having said in his *Philoctetes*:

$$\phi\alpha\gamma\acute{\epsilon}\delta\alpha\iota\nu\alpha\ \mathring{\eta}\ \mu o\upsilon\ \sigma\acute{\alpha}\rho\kappa\alpha\varsigma\ \mathring{\epsilon}\sigma\theta\acute{\iota}\epsilon\iota\ \pi o\delta\acute{o}\varsigma,$$

Euripides has merely altered the $\mathring{\epsilon}\sigma\theta\acute{\iota}\epsilon\iota$ here into $\theta o\iota\nu\mathring{\alpha}\tau\alpha\iota.$[1] Or suppose

$$\nu\mathring{\upsilon}\nu\ \delta\acute{\epsilon}\ \mu'\ \mathring{\epsilon}\grave{\omega}\nu\ \mathring{o}\lambda\acute{\iota}\gamma o\varsigma\ \tau\epsilon\ \kappa\alpha\grave{\iota}\ o\mathring{\upsilon}\tau\iota\delta\alpha\nu\grave{o}\varsigma\ \kappa\alpha\grave{\iota}\ \mathring{\alpha}\epsilon\iota\kappa\acute{\eta}\varsigma$$

to be altered by the substitution of the ordinary words into

$$\nu\mathring{\upsilon}\nu\ \delta\acute{\epsilon}\ \mu'\ \mathring{\epsilon}\grave{\omega}\nu\ \mu\iota\kappa\rho\acute{o}\varsigma\ \tau\epsilon\ \kappa\alpha\grave{\iota}\ \mathring{\alpha}\sigma\theta\epsilon\nu\iota\kappa\grave{o}\varsigma\ \kappa\alpha\grave{\iota}\ \mathring{\alpha}\epsilon\iota\delta\acute{\eta}\varsigma.$$[2]

Or the line

$$\delta\acute{\iota}\phi\rho o\nu\ \mathring{\alpha}\epsilon\iota\kappa\acute{\epsilon}\lambda\iota o\nu\ \kappa\alpha\tau\alpha\theta\epsilon\grave{\iota}\varsigma\ \mathring{o}\lambda\acute{\iota}\gamma\eta\nu\ \tau\epsilon\ \tau\rho\acute{\alpha}\pi\epsilon\zeta\alpha\nu$$

into

$$\delta\acute{\iota}\phi\rho o\nu\ \mu o\chi\theta\eta\rho\grave{o}\nu\ \kappa\alpha\tau\alpha\theta\epsilon\grave{\iota}\varsigma\ \mu\iota\kappa\rho\acute{\alpha}\nu\ \tau\epsilon\ \tau\rho\acute{\alpha}\pi\epsilon\zeta\alpha\nu.$$[2]

Or $\mathring{\eta}\iota\acute{o}\nu\epsilon\varsigma\ \beta o\acute{o}\omega\sigma\iota\nu$ into $\mathring{\eta}\iota\acute{o}\nu\epsilon\varsigma\ \kappa\rho\acute{\alpha}\zeta o\upsilon\sigma\iota\nu.$[3] Add to this that Ariphrades used to ridicule the tragedians for introducing expressions unknown in the language of common life, $\delta\omega\mu\acute{\alpha}\tau\omega\nu\ \mathring{\alpha}\pi o$ (for $\mathring{\alpha}\pi\grave{o}\ \delta\omega\mu\acute{\alpha}\tau\omega\nu$), $\sigma\acute{\epsilon}\theta\epsilon\nu,\ \mathring{\epsilon}\gamma\grave{\omega}$

[1] Aeschylus' line may be rendered 'This ulcer eats the flesh of this my foot'. Euripides wrote 'feasts upon my foot'.

[2] 'I that am small, of no account nor goodly' is by the substitution of more ordinary words lowered into 'I that am little and weak and ugly'; and 'Setting a stool unseemly and table small' into 'Setting a shabby stool and little table'. In both examples the contrast is greater in the Greek. As a parallel illustration in English we might by 'substituting ordinary words' turn 'Sleep that knits up the ravelled sleeve of care' into 'Sleep that relaxes the nervous tension'.

[3] 'The sea-shores roar' into 'The sea-shores croak.'

δέ νυν, 'Αχιλλέως πέρι (for περὶ 'Αχιλλέως), and the like.[1]
The mere fact of their not being in ordinary speech
gives the Diction a non-prosaic character; but Ariphrades was unaware of that. It is a great thing, indeed, to make a proper use of these poetical forms, as
also of compounds and strange words. But the greatest
thing by far is to be a master of metaphor. It is the
one thing that cannot be learnt from others; and it is
also a sign of genius, since a good metaphor implies
an intuitive perception of the similarity in dissimilars.[2]

Of the kinds of words we have enumerated it may
be observed that compounds are most in place in the
dithyramb, strange words in heroic, and metaphors in
iambic poetry. Heroic poetry, indeed, may avail itself
of them all. But in iambic verse, which models itself as
far as possible on the spoken language, only those
kinds of words are in place which are allowable also
in an oration, i.e. the ordinary word, the metaphor,
and the ornamental word.

Let this, then, suffice as an account of Tragedy, the
art of imitation by means of action on the stage.

23–4. *In these two chapters Aristotle compares the art
of drama and the art of epic poetry. In epic, as in drama,
the unity of the story is a point of capital importance. It is
not enough that, like a chronicle, it should relate the events
of a single period or of one man's career. The story must
have 'a beginning, a middle, and an end', the parts must
be subordinate to and coherent in the whole.*

[1] Compare 'I prythee', 'quotha', and all the devices which R.L.S.
described as 'tushery'.

[2] The skill to detect similarity in things not obviously alike is characteristic both of the poet and of the scientist.

Although in Chapter 23 Aristotle says that in the unity of his two epic stories Homer shows his 'marvellous superiority', he admits in Chapter 18 (see p. 52) that the Iliad with its 'plurality of stories' cannot be successfully dramatized and in Chapter 26 (see p. 81) that less unity is required in an epic than in a drama.

On analysis epic poetry is found to have the same species as Tragedy. The plot may be simple or complex (see Chapter 10); its effect may be predominantly due either to character drawing or to tragic 'suffering' (see Chapter 18). But obviously there can be no species of epic, as of tragedy (see Chapter 18), which depends for its effect on 'spectacle'. The constituent elements, also, of an epic are the same as those of a tragedy, with the exception of spectacle and choric song.

An epic poem can be longer than a tragedy and can present events occurring simultaneously at different places, which adds to the richness and variety of interest; and it has another advantage in being able to describe 'marvels' which cannot be represented on the stage. It differs also in metre, since experience has proved that there is only one metre in which epic poetry can be written—the 'heroic' hexameter.

As in his treatment of drama, Aristotle is here also didactic. He keeps in view the application of his theory in practice. And for this purpose he takes Homer as the supreme model of artistic unity, of dramatic construction, of the author's role in epic (he should speak as little as possible in his own character), and above all of the art which is essential both in epic and dramatic poetry, the art of 'telling lies in the right way'.

The effect of Fiction, he tells us, is due to a logical fallacy so used by the author that the reader or spectator accepts without demur events which could not possibly happen. It all depends upon illusion, what Coleridge calls 'a willing suspension of disbelief'. It is futile to present events which are possible or indeed historically true, if in the presentation they are unconvincing. On the other hand we accept Caliban and the Red Queen, the people of Lilliput and Mr. Toad of Toad Hall without questioning their possibility, because by the skilful use of this delectable fallacy they become inherently 'likely'. Probability (i.e. convincingness) is the criterion of success.

23. As for the poetry which merely narrates, or imitates by means of versified language (without action),[1] it is evident that it has several points in common with Tragedy.

I. The construction of its stories should clearly be like that of a drama; they should be based on a single action, one that is a complete whole in itself, with a beginning, middle, and end, so as to enable the work to produce its own proper pleasure with all the organic unity of a living creature. Nor should one suppose that there is anything like them in our usual histories.[2] A history has to deal not with one action, but with one period and all that happened in that to one or more persons, however disconnected the several events may have been. Just as two events may take place at the same time, e.g. the sea-fight off Salamis and the battle with the Carthaginians in Sicily,[3] without converging

[1] i.e. epic poetry.

[2] See Chapters 8 and 9, where the proper principle of unity has already been applied to epic as well as to drama, and distinguished from the unity characteristic of a historical chronicle.

[3] Gelo's defeat of the Carthaginians and the Athenian naval victory over the Persians at Salamis happened in the same year, 480 B.C. Herodotus says they were on the same day.

to the same end, so also of two consecutive events one
may sometimes come after the other with no one end
as their common issue. Nevertheless most of our epic
poets, one may say, ignore the distinction.

Herein, then, to repeat what we have said before,[1]
we have a further proof of Homer's marvellous superiority to the rest. He did not attempt to deal even
with the Trojan war in its entirety, though it was a
whole with a definite beginning and end—through
a feeling, apparently, that it was too long a story to be
taken in at one view, or if not that, too complicated
from the variety of incident in it. As it is, he has
singled out one section of the whole; many of the
other incidents, however, he brings in as episodes,
using the Catalogue of the Ships,[2] for instance, and
other episodes to relieve the uniformity of his narrative. As for the other epic poets, they treat of one man,
or one period; or else of an action which, although
one, has a multiplicity of parts in it.[3] This last is what
the authors of the *Cypria* and *Little Iliad* have done[4].
And the result is that, whereas the *Iliad* or *Odyssey*
supplies materials for only one, or at most two tragedies, the *Cypria* does that for several, and the *Little
Iliad* for more than eight: for an *Adjudgement of Arms*,
a *Philoctetes*, a *Neoptolemus*, a *Eurypylus*, a *Ulysses as
Beggar*, a *Laconian Women*, a *Fall of Ilium*, and a

[1] In Chapter 8.   [2] i.e. the latter half of *Iliad* ii.
[3] But in Chapter 18 Aristotle admits that there is in the *Iliad* also a
plurality of stories.
[4] These lost and certainly inferior epics are only known to us from the
prose summary of Greek Mythology drawn up by Proclus in the fourth
or fifth century A.D. The *Cypria* treated the story of the Judgement of
Paris and the origin of the Trojan War; the *Little Iliad* begins after the
death of Achilles.

Departure of the Fleet; as also a *Sinon*, and a *Women of Troy*.

24. II. BESIDES this, Epic poetry must divide into the same species as Tragedy; it must be either simple or complex,[1] a story of character or one of suffering. Its parts, too, with the exception of Song and Spectacle, must be the same, as it requires Peripeties, Discoveries, and scenes of suffering just like Tragedy.[2] Lastly, the Thought and Diction in it must be good in their way. All these elements appear in Homer first; and he has made due use of them. His two poems are each examples of construction, the *Iliad* simple and a story of suffering, the *Odyssey* complex (there is Discovery throughout it) and a story of character. And they are more than this, since in Diction and Thought too they surpass all other poems.

There is, however, a difference in the Epic as compared with Tragedy, (1) in its length, and (2) in its metre. (1) As to its length, the limit already suggested[3] will suffice: it must be possible for the beginning and end of the work to be taken in at one view —a condition which will be fulfilled if the poem be shorter than the old epics, and about as long as the series of tragedies offered for one hearing.[4] For the extension of its length epic poetry has a special advantage, of which it makes large use. In a play one cannot represent an action with a number of parts

[1] See Chapter 10.   [2] See Chapter 11.   [3] i.e. in Chapter 7, p. 22.

[4] i.e. presumably, at one festival. The number of poets competing at the City festival of Dionysus seems to have been limited to three. Each exhibited three tragedies, and after the end of the fifth century B.C., three Satyr plays. Probably these amounted at one festival to about fifteen or sixteen thousand lines. The *Iliad* contains between sixteen and seventeen thousand lines.

going on simultaneously; one is limited to the part
on the stage and connected with the actors. Whereas
in epic poetry the narrative form makes it possible for
one to describe a number of simultaneous incidents;
and these, if germane to the subject, increase the body
of the poem. This then is a gain to the Epic, tending
to give it grandeur, and also variety of interest and
room for episodes of diverse kinds. Uniformity of
incident by the satiety it soon creates is apt to ruin
tragedies on the stage. (2) As for its metre, the heroic
has been assigned it from experience; were anyone
to attempt a narrative poem in some one, or in several,
of the other metres, the incongruity of the thing would
be apparent.[1] The heroic in fact is the gravest
and weightiest of metres—which is what makes it
more tolerant than the rest of strange words and
metaphors, that also being a point in which the narrative form of poetry goes beyond all others. The iambic and trochaic, on the other hand, are metres of
movement, the one representing that of life and action, the other that of the dance.[2] Still more unnatural
would it appear, if one were to write an epic in a
medley of metres, as Chaeremon did.[3] Hence it is that
no one has ever written a long story in any but heroic
verse; nature herself, as we have said, teaches us to
select the metre appropriate to such a story.[1]

Homer, admirable as he is in every other respect,
is especially so in this, that he alone among epic poets
is not unaware of the part to be played by the poet

---

[1] So too in Chapter 4 we are told that for dramatic dialogue 'Nature
herself found the appropriate metre'.

[2] Cf. Chapter 4, p. 12.

[3] Cf. Chapter 1, p. 5, n. 1.

himself in the poem. The poet should say very little
in propria persona,[1] as he is no imitator when doing
that. The other poets are perpetually coming forward
in person, and say but little, and that only here
and there, as imitators: Homer after a brief prelude brings in forthwith a man, a woman, or some
other Character—no one of them characterless, but
each with distinctive characteristics.

The marvellous is certainly required in Tragedy.
The Epic, however, affords more opening for the improbable, the chief factor in the marvellous, because
in it the agents are not visibly before one. The scene
of the pursuit of Hector would be ridiculous on the
stage—the Greeks halting instead of pursuing him,
and Achilles shaking his head to stop them;[2] but in
the poem the absurdity is overlooked. The marvellous, however, is a cause of pleasure, as is shown by
the fact that we all tell a story with additions, in the
belief that we are doing our hearers a pleasure.

Homer more than any other has taught the rest of
us the art of telling lies in the right way. I mean the
use of a fallacy.[3] Whenever, if A is or happens, a

[1] Homer's manner of representation (see Chapter 3) is 'at one moment
in narrative and at another in an assumed character'. The allusion here is
not to narrative, which is in a sense objective, but to the 'preludes' in
which, speaking in his own character, he invokes the muse.

[2] *Iliad* xxii. 205, 'And to the host divine Achilles nodded with his head
a sign and let them not launch their bitter darts at Hector, lest another
should win glory by shooting him and Achilles himself come second'
(cf. Chapter 17, p. 48, n. 1). It would certainly look odd on the stage.

[3] In the *Rhetoric* Aristotle states the value of this same fallacy, when
insisting on the importance of appropriate delivery, gesture, and diction.
'The mind of the audience commits a fallacy, supposing the orator to
speak the truth, because men *really* situated as he *appears* to be are
affected as he is, so we take it for granted that things are as he says, even
though they really are not.' The fallacy is: If his story were true, he

consequent, B, is or happens, men's notion is that, if
the B is, the A also is—but that is a false conclusion.
Accordingly, if A is untrue, but there be something
else, B, that on the assumption of A's truth follows as
A's consequent, the right thing then is to posit B.
Just because we know the truth of the consequent, we
are in our own minds led on to the erroneous inference
of the truth of the antecedent. Here is an instance,
from the *Bath-story* in the *Odyssey*.[1]

A likely impossibility is always preferable to an
unconvincing possibility. The story should never be
made up of improbable incidents; there should be
nothing of the sort in it. If, however, such incidents
are unavoidable, they should be outside the piece, like
the hero's ignorance in *Oedipus* of the circumstances
of Laïus' death;[2] not within it, like the report of the
Pythian games in *Electra*,[3] or the man's having come
to Mysia from Tegea without uttering a word on the
way in *The Mysians*.[4] So that it is ridiculous to say

would splutter with indignation; but he does; therefore it is true. Similarly
the verisimilitude of fiction rests on, e.g., If we could get through the
looking-glass, we should find a topsyturvy world there; but we *do* find
it vivid and in detail; therefore, the consequent being so convincing, we
wrongly assume the truth of the antecedent.

[1] In the *Bath-story* (*Odyssey* xix) Ulysses approaches Penelope in the
disguise of a Cretan from Gnossos, who had once entertained her husband
on his voyage to Troy; he describes Ulysses' dress, companions, &c.
Penelope argues: If his story were true, he would know these details; but
he does; therefore it is true.

[2] Cf. Chapter 14, p. 38, n. 2, and Chapter 15, p. 43, n. 1.

[3] In Sophocles' *Electra*, the Paedagogus—Orestes' old 'tutor'—gives
a moving and false account of Orestes' death in the chariot races at Delphi.
As the Pythian games had not been instituted in Orestes' time, it may be
that the anachronism offended the critics, or perhaps it seemed unlikely
that the news had not already reached Argos.

[4] A lost play probably by Aeschylus, in which Telephus travelled from
Tegea to Mysia without speaking.

that one's Plot would have been spoilt without them, since it is fundamentally wrong to make up such Plots. If the poet has taken such a Plot, however, and one sees that he might have put it in a more probable form, he is guilty of absurdity as well as a fault of art. Even in the *Odyssey* the improbabilities in the setting-ashore of Ulysses[1] would be clearly intolerable in the hands of an inferior poet. As it is, the poet conceals them, his other excellences veiling their absurdity. Elaborate Diction, however, is required only in places where there is no action, and no Character or Thought to be revealed. Where there is Character or Thought, on the other hand, an over-ornate Diction tends to obscure them.

25. *This is a chapter of critical casuistry. The great age of Greek literature was followed by the epoch of the critics, who flourished like gnats in the climate of Alexandria. They settled in their largest swarms on Homer. Not content with attacking the immorality of his theology, they delighted in making a literal examination of poetic statements, like the statistician who objected to the inaccuracy of Tennyson's lines, 'Every moment dies a man, And every moment one is born.' They insisted that pigs cannot weep, that Aphrodite could not have stooped to set a chair for Helen, and that Nausicaa's 'proposal' to Ulysses was shockingly unladylike.*

In some American universities students who specialize in 'rhetoric' prepare a card index of all the possible objections which may be raised against the points of a speech together with counter-objections and replies. As each ob-

[1] In *Odyssey* xiii Ulysses is landed in Ithaca by his companions while he is still fast asleep.

jection is raised by an opponent in debate, the relevant card is extracted and laid on the table ready for the moment of reply. In much the same way Aristotle here analyses the criticism to which poetry is liable and suggests the lines on which each 'problem'—the word means literally stumbling-block—may be solved, each objection answered.

A poet may in his 'imitation' represent things (1) as they once were, or (2) as they are to-day, or (3) as they are said to be, or (4) as they seem to be, or (5) as they ought to be. Many criticisms are based on a misunderstanding of the poet's intention; it is irrelevant to criticize the romantic idealist because his statements are not true to fact or the realist because his view of life is unpleasant. Other objections may be met by convicting the critic of misinterpretation. He may have misunderstood (6) a rare word or (7) a metaphor; he may have misread (8) the prosody or (9) the punctuation; he may have mistaken the meaning of (10) an equivocal expression, or failed to allow for (11) the custom of language, what we call 'a manner of speaking'. Still more seriously in error, the critic may fail to understand (12) the essentials of poetic truth and to distinguish between the truth of fact and the truth of fiction.

It is under these twelve heads that Aristotle arranges his 'problems' and their solution. The chapter seems queer to modern readers, and it is baffling for those who cannot read Greek, since examples of verbal criticism must inevitably be left in the original language. This presents obvious difficulties both for the interpreter and for the reader. But there is a lot of good fun in the chapter.

25. As regards Problems and their Solutions, one may see the number and nature of the assumptions on which they proceed by viewing the matter in the follow-

ing way. (1) The poet being an imitator just like the
painter or other maker of likenesses, he must necessarily in all instances represent things in one or other
of three aspects, either as they were or are, or as they
are said or thought to be or to have been, or as they
ought to be.[1] (2) All this he does in language, with
an admixture, it may be, of strange words and metaphors, as also of the various modified forms of words,
since the use of these is conceded in poetry.[2] (3) It is
to be remembered, too, that there is not the same kind
of correctness in poetry as in politics,[3] or indeed any
other art. There is, however, within the limits of
poetry itself a possibility of two kinds of error, the one
directly, the other only accidentally connected with
the art. If the poet meant to describe the thing cor-
rectly, and failed through lack of power of expression,
his art itself is at fault. But if it was through his having
meant to describe it in some incorrect way[4] (e.g. to
make the horse in movement have both right legs
thrown forward[5]) that the technical error (one in a
matter of, say, medicine or some other special science),
or impossibilities of whatever kind they may be, have
got into his description, his error in that case is not

[1] See Chapter 2.   [2] See Chapter 21.
[3] This word has a wide meaning in Greek; it covers the whole morality
of social conduct. Thus Oedipus or Othello may have serious faults, yet
be a good 'hero' of poetic drama.
[4] i.e. his original conception may have been incorrect, but if he ex-
presses his conception effectively, his is not an error in art. As Aristotle
says later, it is less sinful in art to represent a hind with horns than to
make it altogether unrecognizable. The fault is not in technique, but in
zoology. The principle may be carried a step farther to meet the criticisms
brought to-day against 'non-representational' art.
[5] It has, but Aristotle didn't know that. Indeed it contravenes his
theories in his treatise on 'How Animals Walk'.

in the essentials of the poetic art. These, therefore, must be the premisses of the Solutions in answer to the criticisms involved in the Problems.

I. As to the criticisms relating to the poet's art itself. Any impossibilities there may be in his description of things are faults. But from another point of view they are justifiable, if they serve the object of poetry itself (what that is has been already stated) and make the effect of some portion of the work more astounding. The Pursuit of Hector is an instance in point.[1] If, however, the poetic end might have been as well or better attained without sacrifice of technical correctness in such matters, the impossibility is not to be justified, since the description should be, if it can, entirely free from error. One may ask, too, whether the error is in a matter directly or only accidentally connected with the poetic art; since it is a lesser error in an artist not to know, for instance, that the hind has no horns, than to produce an unrecognizable picture of one.

II. If the poet's description be criticized as not true to fact, one may urge perhaps that the object ought to be as described—an answer like that of Sophocles, who said that he drew men as they ought to be, and Euripides as they were. If the description, however, be neither true nor of the thing as it ought to be, the answer must be then, that it is in accordance with opinion. The tales about Gods, for instance, may be as wrong as Xenophanes[2] thinks, neither true nor the better thing to say; but they are certainly in

[1] See Chapter 24, p. 68, n. 2.

[2] The philosopher Xenophanes in the sixth century B.C. led the attack on the anthropomorphic religion of the Homeric saga and the immoral behaviour of the Gods. The poet may reply 'I am following tradition'.

accordance with opinion. Of other statements in poetry
one may perhaps say, not that they are better than the
truth, but that the fact was so at the time; e.g. the
description of the arms: 'their spears stood upright,
butt-end upon the ground'; for that was the usual way
of fixing them then, as it is still with the Illyrians.[1]
As for the question whether something said or done
in a poem is morally right or not, in dealing with that
one should consider not only the intrinsic quality of
the actual word or deed, but also the person who says
or does it, the person to whom he says or does it, the
time, the means, and the motive of the agent—
whether he does it to attain a greater good, or to avoid
a greater evil.

III. Other criticisms one must meet by considering the language of the poet: (1) by the assumption
of a strange word in a passage like οὐρῆας μὲν πρῶτον,
where by οὐρῆας Homer may perhaps mean not mules
but sentinels.[2] And in saying of Dolon, ὅς ῥ᾽ ἦ τοι
εἶδος μὲν ἔην κακός,[3] his meaning may perhaps be,
not that Dolon's body was deformed, but that his face
was ugly, as εὐειδής is the Cretan word for handsome-
faced. So, too, ζωρότερον δὲ κέραιε[4] may mean not 'mix

[1] The quotation is from *Iliad* x. 152. It seems a bad way to set up
spears: they might cause an alarm by falling down at night. 'But', the
poet may reply, 'so it was in those days; and the Illyrians do it still.'

[2] *Iliad* i. 50. 'The mules and swift-footed hounds he first beset with his
arrows.' Apollo is sending a plague on the Greeks. Zoilus, 'the scourge
of Homer', ridiculed this as 'small deer for a deity'. The reply is that the
first word may here mean 'sentinels'—but that still leaves the hounds at
the critic's mercy!

[3] *Iliad* x. 316. 'One that was verily evil in form but swift in his run-
ning.' If Dolon was deformed, he could not run fast. But the poet may
only mean that he had an ugly face.

[4] 'Livelier mix it withal.' *Iliad* ix. 202.

the wine stronger', as though for topers, but 'mix
it quicker'. (2) Other expressions in Homer may be
explained as metaphorical; e.g. in ἄλλοι μέν ῥα θεοί τε
καὶ ἀνέρες εὗδον ⟨ἅπαντες⟩ παννύχιοι, as compared with
what he tells us at the same time, ἦ τοι ὅτ᾽ ἐς πεδίον τὸ
Τρωικὸν ἀθρήσειεν, αὐλῶν συρίγγων θ᾽ ὁμαδόν, the word
ἅπαντες, 'all', is metaphorically put for 'many', since
'all' is a species of 'many'.[1] So also his οἴη δ᾽ ἄμμορος
is metaphorical, the best known standing 'alone'.[2] (3)
A change, as Hippias suggested, in the mode of reading a word will solve the difficulty in δίδομεν δέ οἱ, and
τὸ μὲν οὗ καταπύθεται ὄμβρῳ.[3] (4) Other difficulties may
be solved by another punctuation; e.g. in Empedocles,

[1] The two passages here quoted in part are: *Iliad* ii. 1, 2 (quoted in
error for *Il.* x. 1, 2),

　　Thus all the other immortals and all the horse-crested heroes
　　Night-long slumbered, but Zeus the sweet sleep held not . . .

and *Iliad* x, 13, 14,

　　Yea, when indeed he gazed on the Trojan plain Agamemnon
　　Marvelled at voices of flutes and of pipes and the din of the soldiers.

The point is that, if everyone was asleep, who could be making all this noise?

[2] *Iliad* xviii. 489 says of the Great Bear 'She alone of all others shares
not in the baths of the Ocean', i.e. never sets. But there are other con-
stellations which never set. Answer: The Great Bear is the best known;
'best known' is a species of 'alone' (=sole); genus is here metaphorically
substituted for species (cf. Chapter 21, pp. 56–8).

[3] 'Mode of reading' covers pronunciation, intonation, accentuation.
The first quotation is from the beginning of *Iliad* ii, but differs from
the reading in our texts. Zeus sends a 'baneful Dream' to deceive
Agamemnon. To the Dream he says, 'We grant him to win the boast
of great glory.' That puts a lie into the mouth of Zeus. Alter, then, the
accent of pronunciation and the sense becomes 'grant thou him'. It will
then be the Dream, not Zeus, that tells the lie!

The second illustration comes from *Iliad* xxiii. 327:

　　A fathom high from the earth there rises a stump all withered
　　A stump of an oak or a pine, that rots not at all in the rain.

If that seems too much to believe, a change in an aspirate will give
the more credible (but certainly less poetic) sense 'part of it rots in the rain.'

αἶψα δὲ θνήτ᾽ ἐφύοντο, τὰ πρὶν μάθον ἀθάνατα ζωρά τε πρὶν κέκ-
ρητο.¹ Or (5) by the assumption of an equivocal term, as
in παρῴχηκεν δὲ πλέω νύξ, where πλέω is equivocal.² Or
(6) by an appeal to the custom of language. Wine-
and-water we call 'wine'; and it is on the same principle
that Homer speaks of a κνημὶς νεοτεύκτου κασσιτέροιο, a
'greave of new-wrought tin'.³ A worker in iron we call
a 'brazier'; and it is on the same principle that Gany-
mede is described as the 'wine-server' of Zeus, though
the Gods do not drink wine. This latter, however,
may be an instance of metaphor.⁴ But whenever also
a word seems to imply some contradiction, it is necessary to reflect how many ways there may be of understanding it in the passage in question; e.g. in Homer's
τῇ ῥ᾽ ἔσχετο χάλκεον ἔγχος⁵ we should consider the pos-

¹   Soon mortal grew they that aforetime learnt
       Immortal ways, and pure erstwhile commingled.

Empedocles is speaking of elements or atoms. Does he mean that those
which were erstwhile pure became commingled or that those became pure
which were erstwhile commingled? All depends on the reader's pause or
punctuation.

² *Iliad* x. 253.

       Far across are the stars and more than two parts of the night-time
       Gone, but a third is still left us.

This is mathematically impossible. But there is a saving ambiguity. The
meaning may be 'fully two parts of the night-time'.

³ Greaves are made of a compound of tin and copper. But this is in
ordinary parlance called tin, just as a compound of wine and water is
called wine. Similarly 'a whisky' does not necessarily mean neat spirit.

⁴ Nectar: gods:: wine: men. See Chapter 21, p. 56, n. 4.

⁵ The reference is to *Iliad* xx. 272. Achilles is wearing the armour
made for him by the god, Hephaestus, which was in five layers of metal, one
of gold, two of bronze, and the innermost two layers of tin. Homer says
that the spear which Aeneas hurled at him 'drave through two layers and
was stayed in the gold'. But the gold, being ornamental, must have been
on the outside. How then could the spear have penetrated two layers first?
Perhaps, although the point of the spear penetrated the two layers of bronze
underneath, it was the gold on the surface which actually 'stayed' it.

sible senses of 'was stopped there'—whether by taking
it in this sense or in that we shall best avoid the fault
of which Glaucon[1] speaks: 'They start with some improbable presumption; and having so decreed it themselves, proceed to draw inferences, and censure the
poet as though he had actually said whatever they
think he has said, if his statement conflicts with their
own notion of things.' This is how Homer's silence
about Icarius[2] has been treated. Starting with the
notion of his having been a Spartan, the critics think
it strange for Telemachus not to have met him when
he went to Sparta. Whereas the fact may have been
as the Cephallenians say, that the wife of Ulysses was
of a Cephallenian family, and that her father's name
was Icadius, not Icarius. So that it is probably a
mistake of the critics that has given rise to the
Problem.

Speaking generally, one has to justify (1) the Impossible by reference to the requirements of poetry,
or to the better,[3] or to opinion. For the purposes of
poetry a convincing impossibility is preferable to an
unconvincing possibility;[4] and if men such as Zeuxis[5]
depicted be impossible, the answer is that it is better
they should be like that, as the artist ought to improve
on his model. (2) The Improbable one has to justify
either by showing it to be in accordance with opinion,
or by urging that at times it is not improbable; for
there is a probability of things happening also against

[1] Probably an Athenian critic whose views on Homer had high
repute.

[2] The father of Ulysses' wife, Penelope. It seemed strange that their
son Telemachus should not have met him in Sparta (*Odyssey* iv).

[3] i.e. 'things as they ought to be', idealization in the narrow sense.

[4] Cf. Chapter 24, p. 69.   [5] Cf. Chapter 6, p. 18.

probability. (3) The contradictions found in the poet's language one should first test as one does an opponent's confutation in a dialectical argument, so as to see whether he means the same thing, in the same relation, and in the same sense, before admitting that he has contradicted either something he has said himself or what a man of sound sense assumes as true. But there is no possible apology for improbability of Plot or depravity of character[1] when they are not necessary and no use is made of them, like the improbability in the appearance of Aegeus in *Medea*[2] and the baseness of Menelaus in *Orestes*.[3]

The objections, then, of critics start with faults of five kinds: the allegation is always that something is either (1) impossible, (2) improbable, (3) corrupting, (4) contradictory, or (5) against technical correctness. The answers to these objections must be sought under one or other of the above-mentioned heads, which are twelve in number.

26. *The* Poetics *as we have it ends with a comparison of Tragic and Epic poetry. Tragedy may be decried as vulgar, because its appeal is to the crowd and acting can*

---

[1] The characters in tragedy must all be good (cf. Chapter 15, p. 41), and only such faults depicted as are necessary for the outcome of the plot.

[2] When Medea, cast off by Jason, is at her wits' end, Aegeus, King of Athens, suddenly turns up and consents to offer her a refuge. The objection is that this is 'improbable' (see Chapter 15, p. 42) because it is a mere coincidence, uncaused by previous events in the play, and without influence on the result. With the latter point modern critics disagree, and in any case Euripides might retort on Aristotle's own principles 'So it was said to be in the tradition'.

[3] See Chapter 15, p. 41, where Menelaus in Euripides' *Orestes* is cited as 'an instance of baseness of character not required for the story'. Euripides might plead 'The fact was so'.

easily degenerate into monkey-tricks. But that is not the tragedian's fault: besides, epic recitation is sometimes similarly vulgarized. Moreover, acting is not essential for the effect of tragedy, which can be fully felt by a reader.

Tragedy may be preferred, because it contains all the pleasure-giving elements of Epic, with Music and Scenery in addition; its effect on the emotions is stronger because, being shorter, it is more concentrated; it has greater unity; and, lastly, it 'better attains its poetic effect'. What that effect is has been implicit throughout the Poetics *and is clearly stated, e.g. in Chapters 6 and 14, i.e. by a work of 'imitative' art to produce the peculiar tragic pleasure of relief caused by the release of pity and fear and other such emotions.*

Presumably Aristotle would define 'the peculiar epic pleasure' in the same terms and therefore prefers tragedy because its pleasurable effect is on the whole more powerful than that of the epic.

Probably a discussion of Comedy followed in Book II, which was known to exist as late as the 4th century A.D., *but is now lost.*

26. THE question may be raised whether the epic or the tragic is the higher form of imitation. It may be argued that, if the less vulgar is the higher, and the less vulgar is always that which addresses the better public, an art addressing any and every one is of a very vulgar order. It is a belief that their public cannot see the meaning, unless they add something themselves, that causes the perpetual movements of the performers—bad flute-players, for instance, rolling about, if quoit-throwing is to be represented, and pulling at the conductor, if Scylla[1] is the subject of the piece. Tragedy, then, is said to be an art of this order —to be in fact just what the later actors were in the eyes of their predecessors; for Mynniscus used to call Callippides 'the ape', because in his opinion he over-acted his parts; and a similar view was taken of Pindarus also.[2] All Tragedy, however, is said to stand to the Epic as the newer to the older school of actors. The one, accordingly, is said to address a cultivated audience, which does not need the accompaniment of gesture; the other, an uncultivated one. If, therefore, Tragedy is a vulgar art, it must clearly be lower than the Epic.

The answer to this is twofold. In the first place, one may urge (1) that the censure does not touch the art of the dramatic poet, but only that of his interpreter; for it is quite possible to overdo the gesturing even in an epic recital, as did Sosistratus,[3] and in a singing contest, as did Mnasitheus of Opus.[3] (2) That one should not condemn all movement, unless one means to condemn even the dance, but only that of ignoble people[4]—which is the point of the criticism passed on Callippides[2] and in the present day on others, that their women are not like gentlewomen.

[1] Scylla was a water deity with six heads and with legs that were snakes and snarling dogs. We noted in Chapter 1 that Greek instrumental music was accompanied by 'imitative' gesture. In such pieces as Scylla or Quoit-throwing the performers evidently found an opportunity—unequalled even by 'programme music'—for tickling the ears of the groundlings.

[2] Mynniscus was one of Aeschylus' actors; Callippides belonged to the next generation. Pindarus is unknown.

[3] Unknown.

[4] i.e. the representation by gesture and attitude of people of inferior character or class.

(3) That Tragedy may produce its effect even without movement or action in just the same way as Epic poetry; for from the mere reading of a play its quality may be seen. So that, if it be superior in all other respects, this element of inferiority is no necessary part of it.

In the second place, one must remember (1) that Tragedy has everything that the Epic has (even the epic metre being admissible), together with a not inconsiderable addition in the shape of the Music (a very real factor in the pleasure of the drama) and the Spectacle. (2) That its reality of presentation is felt in the play as read, as well as in the play as acted. (3) That the tragic imitation requires less space of time for the attainment of its end; which is a great advantage, since the more concentrated effect is more pleasurable than one with a large admixture of time to dilute it—consider the *Oedipus* of Sophocles, for instance, and the effect of expanding it into the number of lines of the *Iliad*. (4) That there is less unity in the imitation of the epic poets, as is proved by the fact that any one work of theirs supplies matter for several tragedies; the result being that, if they take what is really a single story, it seems curt when briefly told, and thin and waterish when on the scale of length usual with epic verse. In saying that there is less unity in an epic, I mean an epic made up of a plurality of actions, as the *Iliad* and *Odyssey* have many such parts, each one of them in itself of some magnitude; yet the structure of the two Homeric poems is as perfect as can be, and the action in them is as nearly as possible one action. If, then, Tragedy is superior in these respects, and also besides these, in its poetic effect (since the two forms of poetry should give us, not any or every pleasure, but the very special kind we have mentioned[1]), it is clear that, as attaining the poetic effect better than the Epic, it will be the higher form of art.

So much for Tragedy and Epic poetry—for these two arts in general and their species; the number and nature of their constituent parts; the causes of success and failure in them; the Objections of the critics, and the Solutions in answer to them.

---

[1] Cf. Chapter 14, p. 37. 'The tragic pleasure is that of pity and fear and the poet has to produce it by a work of imitation.' Evidently we are to regard the epic pleasure as the same.

PRINTED IN GREAT BRITAIN AT THE UNIVERSITY PRESS, OXFORD
BY VIVIAN RIDLER, PRINTER TO THE UNIVERSITY